P9-CCR-368

WEBSTER COUNTY LIBRARY
P.O. BOX 89
MARSHFIELD, MO 65706

DISCARDED W/CL

Copyright © 2006, 2007, 2008 by Rex Havens

Illustrations Copyright © 2006, 2007, 2008 by Rex Havens

Fourth Printing

All rights reserved. No portion of this book may be reproduced, stored in a retrieval system, or transmitted in any form or by any means whether it be electronic, mechanical, photocopy, or any other, except for brief quotations in printed reviews, without prior permission of the publisher.

Published by Blue River Press, Indianapolis, IN
A Nice Dog Press Production, Bloomington, Illinois 61704.

Nice Dog Press books may be purchased in bulk for business, fund-raising or promotional use. Please call (800) 642-3364 for more information.

Cover Design by Adam Havens

Printed in the United States of America.

Everything I Needed
To Know, I Learned From
MY WIFE!

By
Rex Havens

With Illustrations By
Aaron Warner

WEBSTER COUNTY LIBRARY
P.O. BOX 89
MARSHFIELD, MO 65706

To Sarah:

My favorite and most patient teacher, and the only one I ever kissed. You make the sun rise and my heart dance. OK, you make the sun rise. Even with your love, I still can't dance.

- Rex

Table Of Contents

Foreword

To Men

It takes dignified courage to admit being outmatched, but we must summon the valor to hail our conquerors. If it gives comfort, remember that we admire history's great generals not only for battles won but sometimes for knowing when to quit. Fear not, however, for when certain defeat is honestly faced, a calm, inner peace descends, warming the soul, control is released, one is bathed in serenity, and transported to a place of bliss.

Just like freezing to death.

To Women

Most men beyond the age of 40 know the score. We know this is an Olympics where we scored no medals, a four-game World Series, a roseless Derby with a most unpleasant view. Remember only that, true to our sports ethic, we continue to admire good winners, those who do not gloat, those who are generous in victory, those willing to magnanimously offer hope to all for next season. However slim, leave us some hope for next year. It's what gets us through a long, cold winter.

Please, don't let us freeze to death.

I'm Having The Time Of My Wife

I was a young man once. It didn't work out.

But I was gloriously young, full of myself, confident, and believed fervently, as young men do, that it was a "man's world." I see it today, reflected in the eyes of bold young bucks, embarking on manhood, convinced it is their destiny to control the world and rule all they see. To those young men I offer two thoughts:

First, I admire your optimism.

Second, grow up.

Don't take my word for it, though, young lads. Go out there into the world, struggle, fight. Maybe you are the chosen one. Maybe you are going to succeed where 12 billion men before you have failed.

Then again, maybe not. But give it your best shot.

But on behalf of all the other men who no longer cling to their boyish dream, I'd like to take this opportunity to speak to the women. Now I can only speak as a man, it is the handicap I was born with. But I offer this to you earnestly and in the kindest spirit of healing. I say it with love, honor, respect, affection and all good things. And I think I speak for many men in the world when I say, honestly:

We've tried.

We have tried so very hard to understand you. OK, as best we can with our tiny, underdeveloped little brains. But every time in my life that I thought maybe I understood one small, itty-bitty truth about you women, I think you all call a meeting, take a vote, change the rule. You don't tell the man in your life because that would take the sport right out of it. You leave it up to him to figure out for himself, individually, if he can. Sometimes he does, more often he does not, and the game goes on.

After all these years, it comes down to only two things about men and women which I know are always true. There are only two things I can count on, they're always there for me:

#1 – I'm a man.

#2 – I'm sorry.

Because I have very bad news for the men of America.

Battle of the Sexes? I'm very sorry, it's over, we lost.

I can hear the voices of America's women saying, "Son of a gun. One of 'em finally gets it. Now we're gonna have to call a meeting."

Bad news, gentlemen, indeed. Sometimes I feel we live in a world where the Women's Liberation Movement did its job so well that it may just be time for the Male Surrender Movement?

But take heart, men, we have nothing to be ashamed of. We put up a long, hard, valiant fight . . . and came in second. That's not so bad. After all, second is almost first. When you think about it, we did pretty well. We beat every gender out there, except that one.

From my own valiant fight, I ultimately came to learn that marriage is a democracy — One Woman, One Vote.

I'm told it's not this way everywhere. I understand there are women in the world who are docile, subservient, women who hang on their husband's every word, and treat him like a god. I have never personally met any of these women. Because I live in North America.

And as it turns out, North America is not the ideal environment for the adult male ego to be nurtured and thrive. The male ego. I know it can be a trying and frustrating adversary for many women. I'd like to tell you about the day I lost mine forever.

I was about 40 years old, sitting in my living room, and I was having one of those moments when you count your blessings and appreciate how good life has been to you. Now I don't live in a mansion by any means, but as I sat there, I felt life had been exceedingly kind to me, and I was feeling grateful that day for what I had, my wonderful family, a comfortable home. And as I looked at the things around me — a lifetime-to-date of living room furniture, decorations and mementos — I suddenly realized for the first time that out of everything I was looking at in that room, I had chosen none of it! It hit me like a bolt from the blue. Nothing, nothing, *nothing* I was looking at was there because of some decision I made that it should enter my life and home.

Which was strange to me, because as I thought back to the time I got married, I seem to recall having stuff. In fact, I was fairly confident that, at the time of my nuptials, I was the deeded owner of numerous items of personal property. I could still picture many in my mind. But that was the only place I could still picture them, in the dim, cobwebbed corners of my tiny brain, because now all I could see before me was that they had been gradually, systematically and completely replaced by items of Sarah's choosing.

Sarah, I should explain, is the otherwise bright, witty and beautiful woman whose sole act of unexplained madness was walking down an aisle and reciting marriage vows with me. There can be trouble when someone marries beneath oneself and knows it. Sarah married beneath herself, but she still doesn't know it. And I'm doing my best to keep her in the dark.

But it didn't stop there. I leapt to my feet, full of purpose. I looked in the kitchen – I'd chosen very little of that. I looked in the bedrooms and bathrooms – I'd chosen very little of that as well. I looked in my own closet – I had chosen literally none of that. And ultimately I was rocked yet again, as I realized it was bigger than just the things in my house. Thinking back, I hadn't chosen the house either.

So I started to question for the first time whether I was really the captain of this thing I called my life.

I was sitting in a house I hadn't picked out, surrounded by things I hadn't picked out, eating low-fat chips no male would ever pick out, and I thought to ask myself for the first time: How many battles with the women in my life had I won and lost? I thought of the arguments I'd waged with Sarah and other women over the years. I tried to remember my last argument with a woman which ended with her saying, "OK, you're clearly right, you win." Hmmmm . . . hadn't been that day . . . week, month or year. Turns out no woman had ever said that to me.

So on that fateful afternoon I had a little ceremony, and I laid my male ego to rest. When you're 40 years old and it hits you that you've never won an argument with a woman, honestly, what's the point? So I went to the back yard, held a small service, turned over some dirt, shed a tear, said good-bye to my old ego friend, and faced the world for the first time without him. And today, I no longer have a need to be Macho Man. Instead, at my age, I'm content to sit on the couch with a beer and just be Nacho Man.

I began to understand what a wasteful pursuit it is to try to be macho. It dawned on me that only men talk about "saving face." Women seem to know from the start what most men take their whole lives to learn – nobody's really talking about you, so stop dwelling on your "reputation," because it's so very hard to find someone who wants to do it with you. Most women don't waste time with such things. When's the last time you heard a woman talk about "saving face?" That's right – never. Apparently women learn early on that saving face is a black hole you can pour time and energy into and rarely get anything worthwhile back.

If a woman ever does talk about saving face, she means plastic surgery. As in, "The doctor says that for twenty-five grand, I could save some face."

So I finally put my ego aside and reached the stage in life where I can look myself honestly in the mirror and admit:

Everything I needed to know I learned from my wife.

Now right off the bat, I know not all will agree with me. Some fifteen years ago, as you may remember, a man eloquently wrote that "All I Really Need To Know I Learned In Kindergarten." Really? In kindergarten? Good for him, God bless him – must be a bachelor. Any man who claims he already learned all he needed to know by the ripe old age of six could not possibly be married. I'm willing to concede that kindergarten may teach you many fine things about sharing and playing nice. But I think one could be an honors graduate of kindergarten, maybe even, I dare say, a Phi Beta Kappa graduate of kindergarten, and still in no way be equipped to deal with the stresses of your wife's pregnancy, childbirth, post-partem depression, PMS, menopause and idiot in-laws.

So I believe the lessons you learn after marriage are the most important. And to all prospective husbands-in-waiting, let me say to you that marriage indeed will be the single greatest educational opportunity of your life. Not that you haven't had some education so far. You have, but so far you have been a bachelor, which means all you have today is a Bachelor's Degree. Once you're married you're going for your MMA, a Masters in Matrimonial Arts. They should say that at the ceremony – "I pronounce you husband and wife. Let the lessons begin."

And there will be lessons. By a teacher so vastly accomplished it would make Socrates switch professions and become a shepherd.

But know that this is not a one- or two-semester deal, not a three- or four-year program. This is lifelong learning, 24/7/365, no Spring or Christmas break. There will be seminars, lectures, punishment, reward and numerous pop quizzes.

The training lasts as long as the marriage lasts, and I would encourage you to look at it this way. If you've been married less than 10 years, you're a freshman. 10 to 20 years, sophomore. 20 to 30 years, junior. And finally, after 30 years of marriage, congratulations – you're a senior. Not that you're going to graduate. Even if you've been at it for a solid century, marriage is one school where every man is always a couple of credits short.

"I'm Sorry."
Now Was That So Hard?

The first lesson a new wife teaches her husband is what to do when he screws up. It's important for her to sink this one in early, because screwing up is a husband's full-time occupation. (In his spare time, it's his hobby.) With so many major malfunctions on his horizon, he'll need to be trained quickly so he's ready for his first gigantic snafu, which should be any time now (if it didn't already happen at the wedding), with more to follow on a pace of about one a week for the rest of his natural life.

So the question for the new husband is how to repair the damage and restore peace. If only there were a magic elixer, perhaps a capsule, maybe a shot, even enchanted fairy dust. But there isn't, so forget everything medical science has to offer, fellas, because:

When it comes to mending a strained relationship, nothing holds a candle to the healing power of "I'm sorry."

"I'm sorry" is simultaneously the most powerful marriage mending medicine in history and the hardest pill for some husbands to swallow.

To many people, the soothing power of an apology may seem ridiculously obvious. But men of my generation were blinded to it by a passing cultural phenomenon of our youth. We were blatantly lied to by Hollywood, Ryan O'Neal and Ali MacGraw. Through their carelessness, they doomed millions of marriages. For I blame the movie "Love Story", over 30 years ago, for misleading an entire generation into believing that:

"Love means you never have to say you're sorry."

They even made it into a hit song. Remember?

Love means you never have to say you're sorry? Are you kidding me? Young men, do not go anywhere near a crock that big. It's already over capacity, it could burst at any time, and when it breaks, all your boots put together won't be deep enough.

So listen up, young marriageable males:

Love means you never STOP saying you're sorry.

In fact, love means you should start off each day with a big, fat apology before your feet even hit the floor. For anything you may have done wrong in her dream.

Because, yes, every married man in history has been scolded and punished for fun he did not have! Fun an imaginary him had in her imaginary dreamland. Fun he did not experience and did not enjoy, but for which he must pay. And he must pay because she saw him smiling and laughing and cavorting even while he was actually soundly and innocently sleeping.

Some days her dream is the very reason he wakes up in the first place. No warning, just a sharp elbow to the ribs, as his queen screams, "Do you know what you were doing?" To which he can only reply, "I don't even like your sister."

"Love Story" should have been banned from the theaters, or at least been rated FORBA – Full Of Really Bad Advice. Or PGW for Pathetically, Grossly Wrong. If subject matter can be banned for indecency, then why not for irresponsibility? How can it be legal to give out mass advice which is tantamount to marital suicide?

Erich Segal wrote "Love Story," and his punishment should have been a prolonged public flogging, as many days and years as it took to administer one lash for every relationship he ruined with this uber-tripe. If my guess is correct, he'd still be receiving welts today, around the clock.

Because Erich Segal could not have been more wrong or done a bigger disservice to male/female relations if he had said, "Women like it when you drag them by the hair."

Here's what Mr. Segal should have written:

• Love means, whenever in doubt, say you're sorry. And be constantly in doubt.

• Love means say you're sorry for everything you did, said, thought, omitted, inferred, insinuated, suggested, dreamt, forgot, imagined, deleted, wheezed, whispered, belched or telepathically communicated.

• Love means say you're sorry whether or not you know what

you're sorry for. You did something. If you wait to find out what, it may already be too late.

• Love means sound sincere when you say you're sorry, because if you're not, she'll know, and that's when real sorry begins.

• Love means say you're sorry even if you're positive you did nothing wrong and the whole thing is someone else's responsibility.

That last one is a tough lesson for a man to learn, because he was taught to say "I'm sorry" only when he regrets something he actually caused. In other words, to a man, "I'm sorry" is shorthand for "I'm sorry for what I did."

But to women, "I'm sorry" is a near-universal cure appropriate in numerous settings, many of which have nothing to do with blaming the one uttering the words. It may indeed mean "I'm sorry for what I did," but it can just as easily mean "I'm sorry that happened to you."

For example, "I'm sorry" is an appropriate substitute for all of the following:

• "I'm sorry I did that."

• "I'm sorry he/she/it/they did that."

• "I'm sorry you're upset with me."

• "I'm sorry you're upset with anybody."

• "I'm sorry you're upset about anything."

• "I'm sorry Vanessa wore the same dress as you to the party."

• "I'm sorry the whole world does not know Vanessa had a boob job."

• "I'm sorry Vanessa acts like an upper-crust snob instead of the poor trash she comes from."

• "I'm sorry Vanessa didn't die in a fiery propane accident."

In summary, a husband should learn to say "I'm sorry" any time she's not happy. That's really what it means. "I'm sorry" is just short for "I'm sorry you're unhappy in any way about any little thing in this whole wide world, sweet love of my life, beat of my heart, glow of my cheeks, spring in my step, wind 'neath my wings, fruit of my loom."

"And, oh yeah, one more thing. That Vanessa's gonna get hers."

Chapter 3

A Groom Is Vital To A Wedding Like A Snow Tire Is Vital To A Pizza

Even in light of the advances of women in recent generations, some people still maintain that it's a man's world. Though representing a fading minority, it is still an opinion worthy of respect. Most of us come from free countries, where wars were fought so that people might hold different opinions, and we should celebrate that freedom and never forget how special it is. But if anyone really believes it's a man's world, they owe it to themselves to have . . . a WEDDING.

Yes, indeed, young man, on your wedding day, that is when you will learn your first major lesson, as she and all the circumstances of the day teach you what an incredibly tiny, tiny piece of that day's puzzle you are.

Many grooms make the same mistake. They go into their wedding day thinking to themselves, "Hey, this is MY wedding day. I'm half of the happy couple. Surely this day is at least somewhat in celebration of me."

Sorry, fellas. It's not your day.

Not your day at all.

It's her day. Not your day.

She doesn't even really want you there.

She'd get married without you if she could. The only reason you even got an invitation is there's a law somewhere that says you've got a right to be notified. She may love you and want to be your wife, but trust me, if she could have that beautiful day and just leave you home on the La-Z-Boy, she'd do it every time. To a woman, a wedding is like a ham sandwich – if you're going to have one, unfortunately, somebody's got to invite the pig.

No matter how much she loves you, you're still a man, which means that, on the wedding day, in her mind, you're an accident waiting to happen. You've got to be watched, coached, monitored, rehearsed, spoon-fed, baby-sat and kept sober and on schedule. You will not be trusted with a single major decision about the day – flowers, colors, fabrics, decorations, nothing. She'd like to let you, but frankly, you're too stupid.

You probably won't even be allowed to pick out the clothing you'll wear that day. Perhaps you've been dressing yourself and making your own sartorial decisions for 20 or 30 years by now. But not today. You're just too stupid.

Only she possesses the right sense of composition and proportion to make all the complex design decisions required to make it the perfect presentation, the perfect day.

And let me say I agree completely with letting the bride make these decisions. I fully believe that the average woman has a much better sense of the artistic and the aesthetic than the average man. When I got married, I found out my darling Sarah wanted checks for the checkbook that were – OK, get this – pretty. I'm a man; I just wanted checks that would clear! The way I see it, if I write a check and the bank pays it, that is one beautiful document. That functional little piece of paper did just what it was supposed to do. No pain, no penalty, no "NSF" stamped on it – mission accomplished. The full range of financial beauty as I know it. Whether it looks like a sunrise or a baboon's backside, makes no difference; both are equally beautiful to me and my brethren.

Sarah also informed me we were going to divide the checkbook. I got the deposit slips.

So I say, men, on the wedding day, let her make the decisions, and gladly. Know and respect your limitations. It's her day, not your day. It's the way it's always been and the way it always will be. I make no attempt to change things here, men, and neither should you. It's too much a force of nature, been gathering momentum for too many years. Accept your limited role, know it going in, and things will go better for you.

Everything is about her, as it should be. It starts with the engagement photo in the paper. Who's in the photo? In some papers, they both are, but in others, it's just one. When it's just one, which one? Yes, the bride. Hey, if you're only going to show one, isn't it just common sense it should be the important one?

Next, her gown. The search for it may take weeks, even months. It will cost hundreds, often thousands of dollars. There will be five separate fittings, it must fit perfectly. After the ceremony, her dress will be carefully, lovingly cleaned, pressed, folded, sealed, wrapped in plastic, saved, preserved, treasured, cherished and revered as an altar and shrine for life.

His clothing is rented.

And must be back to the shop on Monday.

Because another guy needs it next weekend.

A minor difference, fellas. Hardly worth mentioning. Don't let it bother you that five hundred other men got married in your suit. Five hundred. That's how many rentals before a tux is so tattered they cannot in good conscience rent it to one more guy. Five hundred wearings. But you're still special.

Fifty years from now the bride can hold up her gown and say, "I got married in that." If the groom can do that, he'll be holding underwear.

Chapter 4

I've Got The Wedding Bell Dues

A groom can learn a lot about his new life by studying the jewelry of marriage.

The bride's ring stops traffic. Everyone wants to see it, gasp at it, talk about it, know all the details of size and cut and the story of how he gave it to her.

And this ring is incredible. You're supposed to spend three month's income on her ring. Know who says so? The American Diamond Association. What a shock.

Now I spent three months income on Sarah's ring, and she was still mad. I chose June, July and August from the summer I turned thirteen. It was my money, so I thought I got to pick the time frame. I figured I had a loophole. Apparently not.

Her ring is amazing, a thing of sculpted, precise beauty. Thousands of dollars.

His ring? $82.50. Most stores throw it in when you buy hers.

It's the jeweler's way of saying, "Hey, fella, we ripped you off on that rock pretty bad. Whatya say this piece of junk's on the house. No, please, take it. Here, take six or seven, we got 'em in a bucket back here. Take a fistful, go ahead. Wear one on your foot if you like. Really. They don't cost us nuthin'. We use 'em for packing peanuts. You deserve it. You're a good boy."

Diamonds are a girl's best friend.

Man's best friend is a dog.

Who thought that up? *Women* thought that up.

Who else could have come up with that? Woman's best friend is one of the most beautiful, precious, extraordinary things on the planet. Man's best friend is so plentiful we neuter them because we don't want more.

It's very hard to get woman's best friend – it's three miles down in an African diamond mine. Where do we get man's best friend? "My neighbor had an extra, he gave it to me. He was just gonna shoot it, so I took it off his hands. Price was right. He's my buddy."

Gentlemen, we must face facts. They beat us on this one. Women have a best friend over which nations have waged wars and for which airtight security must be vigilantly maintained. Man's best friend leaves behind "presents" nobody is happy to receive. Presents left around so carelessly and abundantly we actually step in them. Personally I'd like to stop observing whatever holiday these presents are for.

But now let's risk making the women angry. Because it's time to reveal a secret about their "best friend" which women have managed to keep under wraps for centuries, and which they'd probably like to keep buried indefinitely. Ready?

Diamonds are not actually rare.

In fact, by all evidence, far from it. Diamonds are apparently quite abundant, and probably not worth anywhere near what men have been convinced to pay for them.

Don't believe me? Think I should be tortured with a thousand sharp ends from a thousand Cartier ear studs? Then consider this: If something is rare, shouldn't there occasionally be shortages?

It's perhaps the most basic rule of the marketplace. If something is truly rare, there will be times when you can't get it, find it or buy it, not at any price. In fact, that's what "rare" means — "not always obtainable."

But ask yourself, in your entire life, have you ever walked into a jewelry store and been told, "Sorry, we're out."? Have you ever left the house intent on a diamond purchase, only to come home empty-handed, with the explanation that, "Unfortunately, even though the miners are working triple shifts, they just haven't found any this month."?

Not me. In fact, I've never been to a big mall that didn't have at least six jewelry stores, with not a single empty display case, not even a single empty slot in a case to be found among the whole lot of them. Every display unit full, more in the back, more coming tomorrow, more next week, don't worry, if you want it, it's here, and it's yours. If diamonds were any less scarce, the mall would be nothing but jewelry stores, with Foot Locker and The Gap evicted as homeless orphans forced to operate out of the trunk of a Chevy.

In contrast, I have seen merchants run out – dead out – of strawberries, melons, grapefruit, canola oil, coffee, eggs, bread, sugar and syrup. Impending natural disasters cause runs on cereal and Fruit Roll-Ups. International trade snags foster the occasional paper shortage. I've lived through times when I couldn't buy gasoline. Heck, in the middle of January I've even seen stores be out of rock salt and snow shovels. But I've never seen jewelers be even so much as low on diamonds, a commodity so hopelessly rare it's always available.

Come to think of it, we've heard predictions for the last 30-40 years that the world has only enough oil for another 30-40 years. Ever heard a forecast on how many more years before we harvest the last diamond? It has to be out there, doesn't it? The world's last diamond, waiting to be unearthed? Could it be our generation should quit buying them so there'll be some left for our grandchildren?

I suggested that to Sarah. She told me to get busy. Because she said if the world's last diamond is really out there waiting to be found, and I'm not the guy who finds it . . .

Nah, she was kidding. I think.

Somebody's Got To Tell A Newly-Married Man Where He Stands

So now, my young groom friend, your wedding day has arrived. You've put a rock that cost more than your first two cars on her hand, she's picked out your tux, and the magic day is here. Try your best to stop throwing up, it's going to be great. Yes, it's her day, but that doesn't mean you can zone out. Your lessons have begun and are in full swing, so pay attention. Otherwise final exams will be the same nightmare they were in high school.

One important lesson was months ago, because you may have noticed that once you were engaged, you had to "register." This surprises most men. "Register? You mean like a handgun?" No, no, not with the state, with the stores. You "register" for the gifts you want people to buy for you. And by "you" we mean "her."

Because all grooms learn this: The happy couple only registers for feminine things.

You register for china, linen, silver and crystal. You never register at the liquor store, the gun shop or the pool hall. There will never be any Hooter's gift certificates in those packages, no matter how thoughtful, generous and appreciated that might be.

It's her day, dummy. You'll learn she gets her own carpet for the ceremony. I envy that. What a nice touch. They wait until the last moment when she's about to enter, then – whoosh – they unroll her own very special carpet. The carpet's not for the groom. You only get to walk on it if you first go through with the ceremony, then only on the way out, and only by her side. Other than that, fella, stay off the rug. Pretty good rule for the rest of the marriage, too. Stay off the rug, big guy. It can only turn out badly.

Her day. She gets a veil. What a note of elegance. After all, her face is the central visual gift of the day, and her loveliness will eventually be shared and admired by the beloved guests. But first, to maintain suspense, her face is delicately veiled, so that she may glide down the aisle in stately mystery, arrive at the altar, where she is dramatically unveiled, and everyone gasps at her beauty.

The groom's face? It's at the end of his neck, just like always. No special day for his face. Sorry, pal.

Her day. Her entrance into the church is magical. Everyone stands, everyone turns, there is special music, all because the bride is almost here. And even then, the anticipation must build as she first sends in the bridesmaids. Someone in the crowd (always a man) gets confused when the first woman he sees is not the bride. "Honey, that's not Susan. I know that's not her. Are we in the right church? . . . What? Oh, I get it, sample women first. Bride appetizers. OK, I'm with the program now. Bring 'em on down."

And each bridesmaid is doing that time-honored, halting,

staggered, one-baby-step-at-a-time Wedding Walk. You know the one. Like your dog right after he got fixed.

That's her entrance, and it's truly grand, breathtaking, sentimental and timelessly memorable. And the groom's entrance? A little less. The clergyman explains it to him at rehearsal. "OK, Jim, now tomorrow, son, we'd like you to come in through the alley door over here. Just come in quiet-like at no particular time when nobody gives a rip, that's how we do it here. Don't attract attention to yourself. Just drag your little puppy-dog-tail self to the center here, and if you do it right, the whole crowd will look up and say, 'Where the heck did he come from? Doesn't he at least get a bell or a whistle? Nothing?'"

On the biggest day of a man's life, he'll be standing in an alley next to a dumpster with hungry cats at his feet. His friends are handing him the keys to a Nissan so old it's a Datsun.

(Because that's the rule in most households. It's the man's job to drive the bad car. It's true in over 90% of marriages. She drives the new, comfy car – he drives the sputtering death trap with no air conditioning or radio. He drives to work singing the Husband Song. "Yeah, I'm a married man, married man, married man. I got a ring and a thermos and a rusty car, I'm a married man, married man, married man." In the parking lot at work, he waves to guys in other rusty cars. "Hey, Bill, ya got 400,000 miles on that thing yet? Gee, Tony, is that new? Wow. Nice thermos! How can he afford that? I bet he's makin' payments.")

Learn this, fellas, and it puts it all in perspective. There's a "special song" for her entrance, and it is in fact popularly called "Here Comes The Bride." Red alert: There is no special music for your entrance. Nothing. Never been even one written, not in all the history of music. And by now you'd think there would be a song about literally everything. Millions of composers writing for millions of years.

There are songs about trains, shipwrecks, Chevrolets, GTO's, little Nash Ramblers, little deuce coupes, bubble gum, suede shoes, Love Potion #9, lollipops, doing it my way, doing the twist, doing the monster mash, doing drugs, doing time and doing it in the road. Songs about fame, fortune, the grapevine, don't sleep in the subway, that voodoo that you do, streakers, roller derby and Doo-Wah-Ditty-Ditty-Dum-Ditty-Do.

Songs about Georgia, San Jose, San Francisco, New York, Chicago, Houston, Kokomo, Paris, London, Tokyo, Shanghai, Santa Catalina, singin' in the rain and walkin' in Memphis.

Not to mention songs about dying, crying, lying, flying, buying, spying, prying, trying and sighing. Tributes to rock & roll, rocka-billy, rocket man, jailhouse rock, rocky top, rock around the clock, love you like a rock, big rock candy mountain and the big bad rock of ages. The magic touch, magic man, black magic woman, this magic moment, do you believe in magic and Puff the Magic Dragon.

Odes to Dolly, Rhonda, Layla, Sharona, King Tut, Sloopy, Mame, Barbara Ann, Bill I love you still, a boy named Sue, and girls with nothing more going for them than junk in the trunk.

All Renee had to do was walk away and she got a song. Some girl from Ipanema got a song, and nobody even knows her name. Not that lack of a name makes her unique, because there are songs about a brown-eyed girl, a devil in a blue dress, a "pretty woman" and girls who just wanna have fu-un. Heck, some "horse with no name" got both a song and the title! And some no-name guy got a song for doing nothing more than to just drop in to see what condition his condition was in.

So you'd think everybody would have a song by now, and not merely the just and virtuous. Even Leroy Brown has a song, and he's bad. Bad. B-b-b-b-bad to the bone.

But turn over every last page of sheet music ever written and you'll not find a single tune devoted to the fact that a groom is about to walk to the altar. Lay, lady lay across my big brass bed, but nary a note for a man to be wed.

And there probably never will be. Because what could they call it?

"Show Up, Shut Up & Smile"?

She's The Focus.
Get The Picture?

Her day. Got it yet?

I want to say, from the heart, that if I could press a button and be a woman for a year, I'd do it at the drop of a hat.

I would love to understand the depth of friendships that women have for each other. I believe it's deeper than any two men have ever known.

Gentlemen, have you ever seen what it's like when one woman asks another to be in her wedding? This is simply and absolutely the greatest excitement any two people on this earth can share. Light years beyond any two guys high-fiving each other at any Super Bowl celebration ever. If you've ever witnessed it, you know it is beyond description. There is just nothing like the moment when one woman looks deep into the eyes of her good friend, eyes wide as basketballs, arms flailing, gasping for breath, as she lovingly squeaks:

"Wait, wait, wait . . . . . Are you ready for this? . . . . . wait, wait, wait, wait, wait, wait . . . . I don't believe it . . . . . wait, wait . . . . . . sit down, sit down . . . . I want . . . I want . . . . *I want*

45

you to be in the wedding!"

And the friend, lovingly and on cue, wets herself.

"OOOOOOOOOOOHH! I'm so HAPPY for you!!! This is toooo wonderful! I LOVE you so much! Geeeez, there's so much to do! Oooh, oooh, what are your colors, WHAT ARE YOUR COLORS??!!"

I ask you, who in their right mind wouldn't want to be in on that? Anybody not enjoy celebrating? Surely not. Celebration, by definition, is fun. And everybody loves fun, because it's so much fun.

And what a tremendous celebration it is. The running and jumping and kissing and hugging, for the honor – no, the privilege – of spending $500 on the ugliest dress you've ever seen in your life. After three or four bridal showers, this wedding will easily cost each bridesmaid a grand. But they don't care. They're honored, and happy, because they truly love their friend that much.

It's not the same for the groom. He walks into work on Monday: "Hey, Tom . . . aw, man, I hate to do this. But . . . I got . . . I got eleven spots to fill. Nah, they had a meeting, that's all I know, and it's eleven. Got word over the weekend, it's in stone, no changing it. And, look, I know we haven't hung around for a few years, but I've always thought of you as my eleventh best friend. Me? I'm Ralph from accounting, I thought you remembered me. We played softball that time? Anyway, what I'm trying to say is . . . well, I need you to stand up with me."

His "friend's" reaction? "Oh, man, that's SIXTY BUCKS! Oh, man!

Isn't there anybody else you can nail this one on? You got a paperboy, don't you, or a cousin, maybe somebody from grade school? How 'bout that guy in the park, 'Will work for food'? Oh, cripes! There'd better be an open bar, that's all I'm sayin'. I see a cash bar, I'm walkin' and you won't catch me. Open bar, at least I can break even. Oh, I can drink back a tux rental, done 'er before."

Her day. The clergyman asks, "Who gives this woman to be married to this man?" Again, she's cherished and protected as a precious asset. Her family gets to decide if she goes or stays.

Her father, who just handed the bride off at the altar, now sits there conferring with her mother, asking, "Honey, whadya think? Should we keep her or give her to dipstick over there? You think he's all right? Never liked him myself, how 'bout you? I think there's a time limit, sweetheart, reverend seems to want an answer. Ah, well . . . OK . . . her mother and I do."

The groom's family, on the other hand, is not consulted at all. It is presumed they are delighted anyone wants him in the first place. His family's over there saying, "Yeah, let her wash his dirty shorts for a while. We'll see how love blooms in that fertilizer."

And there the new couple stands, before a person of the cloth, who "pronounces" them husband and wife. That's right, you get "pronounced" husband and wife. One of only two times in this world you get "pronounced" something.

Married and dead.

It may not sound comforting, but it is what we say. Some

people get "pronounced" married, and, unfortunately, others get "pronounced" dead. But it makes sense, because they're very similar experiences. For either way, people pray, people cry, and they haul you off in a nice car.

So the deed is done, and now you're Man and Wife. Mr. and Mrs. Mister – "M-R" – two letters. Missus – "M-R-S" – three letters. Gentlemen, her title is 50% bigger than yours. Shouldn't that have been a clue?

(Not that you have to be married for this kind of thing to occur. Just ask Brad Pitt. When he and Angelina became an item, the press quickly dubbed the new hot couple "Brangelina." Notice how Brad lost 25% of his original name, while Angelina kept all of hers? Any man out there think he's cooler than Brad Pitt?)

You're man and wife now. Time to break in some new vocabulary. Marriage has its own terminology, and the groom has to get up to speed, and quickly.

For example, Mr. Newlywed, your new wife will henceforth be referred to as your "better half." As in, "Boss, I'd like you to meet Nancy, my better half." "Better half." You're part of a team now, fella, a team with two halves. The team has a better half – and she's it. But by definition that means the team necessarily has a lesser, embarrassing, inferior half. Welcome to the party, son.

Man and wife. My schooling started immediately, right at the reception. I hadn't been married more than an hour before I was staring into the face of Lesson One For The New Husband.

Everyone wanted to take photos. Sarah, my new wife, the

Blushing Bride, was in all of them. Sarah was in constant demand. No camera flash lit up without her smiling face center stage in front of it.

I, on the other hand, was in, well, some of them. We had been wed, had become one, but it turned out to be really more like she was the USA to my Canada, in that we shared a common language but I knew the rest of the world thought I was a bit odd and didn't really know what to do with me. Every shot started with Sarah, and built from there. I only entered the frame after someone said something like, "Oh, why don't you get in there for this one, too?"

Lesson Two followed immediately at the punch bowl. The hostess handed Sarah two cups of punch, but as Sarah turned to me, she looked disdainfully down into one of them and said, "Oh, darn it, this one's got a fly in it." And without a moment's moral hesitation, she extended an arm and gave me the bad one. Her innate, bridely reaction: "Oooh! Contaminated! Icky! Yours!" My reaction was equally innate. I accepted it, fished out the offending floater, and drank it. I was a husband now: "Oooh! Contaminated! Icky! Yummmm!"

Seven Things Husbands Should Learn To Say

I learned from my wife that men and women don't use the same language rules.

Alas, we poor, dull males are mired in a communication mindset which sabotages any hope we might have to be on the same frequency as our wives. Because men believe that after we've said something once – one time – then it's out there, as good as in stone, past our own lips, from our own mouths, on the record, established, for all to know, and permanently embedded in the minds of all who heard it. Those were our male words, we said them, we meant them, we stand by them. End of story.

But odds are, fellas, your wife doesn't work that way. And she wishes you didn't either.

Let's say she comes home after a marathon session at the beauty shop. New hairdo, color change, possibly a skin treatment to restore that youthful "glow." She has a happy, expectant look on her face when she walks in the house. And you're a considerate guy, you know where she went, you can see she's waiting for some word from you, and you respond. "You look great, honey. I love what they did!"

And you're proud of yourself. That was an opportunity to succeed or fail, and you soared. Another man might have dropped the ball, but not you. You said the right thing at the right moment with the right tone. Victory. You contemplate rewarding yourself with a beer, even though it's only 11 AM.

You consider it a job well done, and therein lies your mistake. The job is not done, only begun. What many men fail to realize is that the compliment you gave her so convincingly at 11 AM has a shelf-life of no more than 90 minutes. Tops.

This news is shocking to a man, I know. It is literally inconceivable to the male mind. But trust me, gentlemen, by 12:30, it will be as though you never said a thing. Those praiseful, thoughtful words you were so proud of are on their last legs, and will expire, unless renewed. The stone tablet you thought you had inscribed them on is rapidly crumbling to sand, and you must take up your chisel again, and pronto.

Find a way, and do it. Think of something. Say to one of the kids at lunch, "Doesn't your Mom look great?" There, wasn't that easy? Five little words. One quick breath. And with it, you just bought yourself another 90 minutes.

But 2 PM's approaching. As she walks by, suddenly blurt out, "When's the salon gonna take back this young schoolgirl and bring back my wife?" Now you're golden till 3:30. Nice going. Hey, now's not too early for a beer, is it?

Keep this up for the first day, at least. Whether treatment needs to continue into a second day or beyond will vary, so be alert and don't let your guard down until you're sure it's safe. Then have two beers, no matter what time it is.

Though women don't like to be seen as vain, most unquestionably are, and Sarah is no exception. No matter what the situation, she always wants to know how she looks. Like the last time I asked her to make me a sandwich, and she came back with, "Do I look like a short-order cook?" See what I mean? I'm hungry, and all she cares about is what she looks like. Or I'll ask her to wash my jeans and she'll say, "Do I look like your maid?" I don't get it. How does my desire for clean clothes lead to a discussion of her appearance? Go figure, but that's Sarah for you.

Women aren't vain? Heck, the place where they get ready is actually called a "vanity." Life doesn't get much more obvious than that. Not vain? Sarah thinks Labor Day is to honor women for giving birth.

Women, please try to understand that the reason it's so hard to get men to grasp the concept of the continuing compliment is that not only are men trained to believe that once something's been said there's no need to say it again, but men are also conditioned to believe that if words do have to be repeated, there may be severe consequences. Many of our fathers brought us to laser-beam attention with the warning, "I'm not going to tell you again!" Followed shortly by a beating, which was an earlier and more physical version of time-out.

Among male friends, saying something once is always enough. If a guy tells his friend, "You're the best stickball player on the block," that friend will never forget those words, or let the one who said them forget it. Ever. They might even make it onto his headstone.

Repeatedly compliment a man about the same thing every few hours, and he'll get tired of hearing it, sometimes to the point of being physically uncomfortable. "Enough already. Change the subject. Thanks, but let's talk about something else."

That's because compliments between men never expire. If a man says it, he means it, and he means it for all time. Remember, it's only a woman's prerogative to change her mind. Men, on the other hand, are stuck with their pronouncements, both the wise and the foolish. But only for eternity.

So I learned from my wife that encouraging words need to be repeated periodically, or they lose their potency.

And these kind words don't have to be excessive or over-the-top to be effective. One of the great love songs of my youth was "Pearly Shells" by Don Ho, and it made women go limp, they thought it was so romantic. Here are the lyrics:

> "Pearly shells, from the ocean,
> Shining in the sun, covering the shore.
> When I see them, my heart tells me that I love you,
> More than all the little pearly shells."

Men, do you get it? You don't have to tell them you love them more than life itself, or you'd die in a raging fire for one last kiss from their sweet lips. Far from it. Many women are perfectly happy if you just tell them you love them more than shells.

So I went in search of the most important statements and phrases useful to the modern husband. I wanted to learn what are the key words a good man should say to a good woman if he wants to keep her for a good long time. It was a long and grueling search, but after years of patient and painful observation, I compiled seven items of wisdom (many difficult for men to say) which kept rising above the others.

Gentlemen, this may be bitter medicine, but it's important. Learn to say these if you have a good woman you'd like to grow old with:

1. "You were right — I was wrong."

2. "I'm sorry and that won't happen again."

3. "How could I be so stupid?"

4. "I don't deserve you, sweetheart."

5. "I would marry you all over again."

6. "No, you're much prettier than she is."

7. "No, if anything that dress makes your butt look too small."

And, as an expansion of #7, if necessary: "Really, honey, you should eat something. You're just about to blow away. I don't even know how your slacks stay on your hips. There just isn't any meat for 'em to grab onto!"

I learned #7 the hard way.

Now make no mistake – I love Sarah to death. She will always be the best thing that ever happened to me, I have no idea why such a fine woman would stay with the likes of me, and I shall keep her as long as she is misguided enough to stay.

But one day Sarah ambushed me with a question, and I didn't have time to – what do they call that? – "think." She said, "Will you still love me when I'm fat and sassy?"

And I said, "You're not thinkin' about turnin' sassy on me, are you?"

In the world of trial and error, that was an error. Huge error!

In fact, gentlemen, allow me to advise that when you are tempted to make a snappy comeback like that to something she says, you are being faced with what I call a split-second "Wife-or-Death" decision.

You can understand a lot about our differences by the way each gender reacts to that joke the many times I have told it. The general male reaction to "You're not thinking about turning sassy on me?" is one of respect, approval and applause. "Oh, that's a good one. Clever, well done. You fought valiantly, brave knight." Yet it's also one of the strangest laughs you'll ever hear. It's an odd combination of "That was severely clever, yet at the same time suicidally stupid."

But women boo – and loudly. Even more, I have had popcorn, napkins, pretzels, pizza and ice hurled at me over the years by women who are, in essence, saying, "You are a dead man!" And I completely love that about women. They care about Sarah, even though they've never met her. But they sense one of their own has been wounded. And that's enough. So they circle the wagons, and they say with one voice, "We're gonna get him!"

Women, be proud, be very proud of that instinct. It elevates you. A man seldom cares about another man he's never met. A man will laugh hysterically at his own best friend, caught in some humiliating situation – perhaps just having walked through a plate glass window (lots of mess and at least some blood, yes, that's a good one) – twisting in the wind. A man will laugh and point and call over others to share in his best friend's misery. "Oh, man, you are an idiot! Fellas, come look at this fool over here. You guys ever see such a loser? We're having T-shirts made. You are the moron of the century, my friend. I love ya buddy, but you had yer head way up yer keester. Wait. Yes! That's what we'll print on the T-shirts. 'Bill really had his head in his glass on that one!'"

So to all the women over the years who have run to Sarah's defense when I've told the "fat and sassy" joke, let me commend you for your heart and compassion, but let me also assure you that Sarah does not need your protection. She's a very strong woman, and she can and does take very good care of herself. She still tells everyone that, years ago, the instant she agreed to marry me, she looked down and saw that her hands were suddenly all skinned up and rough. Because, well, that's what happens when you "scrape" the bottom of the barrel.

Chapter 8

A Guy's Guide To Wife Gifting

Nothing delivers mental anguish to even well-intentioned husbands more than worrying over what birthday or Christmas present will completely touch her heart. This is important because men know that a gift which touches her heart leads to husbands touching their wives. Men also know that women talk to each other and compare dumb gifts they've received in the past, and laugh at the idiocy of the stupid, stupid, stooooopid husbands that gave them these "gifts", and no man wants to be the next pig on the spit.

The champion so far in my experience was the woman who told me her husband gave her a Christmas backhoe. She was not a member of the heavy construction industry, but by strange coincidence, he was. On Christmas Eve he secretly drove the backhoe into the driveway and tied a big red ribbon around it. Then on Christmas day he walked her outside with her eyes shut tight, yelled "Surprise," and showed her what he had Caterpillar make for "her." And he expected her to be happy about it! That guy made it all the way to the Clueless Hapless Hopeless Gropeless Husbands Hall of Fame.

Most men don't have great imaginations when it comes to

shopping for women. We seldom leave the house with a target gift in mind. Rather, we troll the malls and shops waiting for "it" to magically appear, reach out and grab us.

The problem is, sometimes what reaches out and grabs us is a space-age-looking Black & Decker toaster oven.

Note to untrained, raw recruit husbands: Never, never bring home a Christmas gift made by Black & Decker. No matter how much in speaks to you in the store. No matter how stylish it looks. Whoever Black and Decker are, they do not make any products which make wives get all weak in the knees. The same goes for Sunbeam, Oster, General Electric, Hoover, Singer and Oreck. If the household needs a new vacuum, buy it, but do NOT make it a gift. I know it costs more overall when you can't get a two-fer with a "gift" that's also an essential, but find the money, rob a store if you must. No matter how sexy those NAPA jumper cables look, no matter how much she needs them in her trunk, do not try to pass them off as a present.

What makes a good gift for a wife? Simple, just three words:

1) Silly
2) Unnecessary
3) Extravagant

That's the whole ball game, gentlemen. No more ammo needed. If a husband will just go to the mall with those three words in his head, and buy anything which is all three, he's in. He must, of course, apply male standards to the task. Don't use female guidelines, because to wives these same items are essential, mandatory and worth every last penny.

So, gentlemen, if you find yourself mid-December at Penney's staring at a Hamilton Beach fruit juicer, go down the mental list. "Silly? Unnecessary? Extravagant?" Wow. Oh-for-three. Run!

On the other hand, if you're holding a string of black pearls, do it again. "Silly? Sure. Unnecessary? Of course. Extravagant? Good Gaaawd!!" Then to the sales clerk, "I'll take these, please. Wrap 'em up." Hand over your car title as payment and you're good to go.

A man's best bet, if he wants to avoid running down the List of Three each time, is to shop exclusively in stores which carry only items satisfying all three criteria. Conveniently, some retailers carry only merchandise which all husbands view as silly, unnecessary and extravagant. Safe bets are Tiffany, Coach, Louis Vuitton, Zale's, Armani, Rolex, Ralph Lauren, Lexus, Faberge and De Beers.

Warning, gentlemen, don't get too excited about "De Beers." It's not what you think.

Chapter 9

His 15 Minutes and Her 15 Minutes Are Not The Same

"We need to drop by the mall for just a minute."

I remember the first time Sarah said those words to me. I remember because I believed her. We needed to drop by the mall "for just a minute." I am a man, which means I take things literally. My wife and I were going to the mall for one minute.

I did not know what could be accomplished at the mall in so little time, but I trusted this must be some sort of special mission. Perhaps there was a sales clerk with a package standing by one of the doors and we would whoosh by and pick it up, like a Pony Express rider snagging a bag of mail. Maybe a quick trip to a drive-up ATM. Maybe she was dropping a payment off in a box. I was just glad we weren't going to be there long. I was so overjoyed I wasn't going to complain even if it took two minutes.

That was the day I learned what "a minute" means to my wife. Because in that "minute," I ate two mall meals, found the men's room in four department stores and took a chair nap in Ladies' Lingerie. If Sarah's "minute" was the real definition of a minute, then the average human lifespan would be about six weeks.

Which is not to say that she was ignorant or oblivious to what she said. She knew she said a minute, and she knew it would be five hours. But she was dealing with a husband, and that means sometimes disguising the truth is required. Because a husband might agree to go to the mall if he's told it's just for a minute, but no husband would go near the car if his wife said, "Whatya say we go shopping for five hours?" His old war wound would flare up at that point, even though he was never in the military.

Thinking back, some of our biggest adjustments as newlyweds were over differing interpretations of time.

"I'll be ready to go in fifteen minutes," she'd call from the bathroom. I believed her.

Silly rabbit.

But for the longest time I took her at her word, I'd look at my watch, and fifteen minutes later I'd be standing in the foyer, holding the front door open, waiting. And waiting. And waiting and waiting and waiting.

Looking back, I don't know how I could have been so foolish. No human could do in fifteen minutes what she needs to do to get ready to leave the house. Because in fifteen minutes one simply cannot wash, blowdry and style one's hair, mend and paint twenty nails, try on thirteen different outfits, apply makeup, walk through a cloud of perfume, sew on a button, curse at and toss out the first pair of pantyhose, pull on the second pair, talk to her mom on the phone, tweeze eyelashes, coordinate bags with shoes with jewelry and still make it to the front door in one beautiful piece. Seventy-five minutes, maybe. Fifteen minutes, forget it.

But I'm smarter today, and I now have a system. I say to her, "Let me know when you start looking for your purse." And when she gives me that word, I begin to get ready. Without any rush at all, I'll still have time to rise from my chair, shave, shower, dress and beat her to the car.

And don't even get me started on, "Could you come in here for just a second?" It took me six months to remodel that kitchen.

The first time I heard "The Scream" I knew instantly a crazed, axe-wielding murderer had broken into our home and was about to hack my sweet wife to death.

My heartbeat tripled, I sprang to my feet, I attacked the stairs three at a time to defend my fair queen. I was not armed, but I would fight this monster with bare hands if necessary. I would overtake him with a powerful rush, wrestle him to the ground and beat him senseless. This was one deranged maniac who had made the mistake of messing with the wrong house.

I rounded the corner to confront my nemesis, foaming at the mouth, charged up like Hulk Hogan on angel dust. There was no trail of blood, so perhaps "The Scream" had kept him (naturally I assumed the killer was a man) at bay. My defining moment as a new husband was at hand as I arrived panting at ground zero.

But there was only Sarah, standing on top of the toilet tank, clutching the drapes for balance. There was no escapee in prison garb, flashing a demented smile, swinging a rusty blade. There was, in fact – nobody. Just Sarah, still screaming, trembling, terrified, quaking, frozen. And pointing. Pointing at the sink.

"KILLLLL IT!" she pleaded.

"Who?" I asked.

"KILLLLLLLLL IT!"

"Where?"

"KILLLLLLLLLLLLLLLLL IT!!!"

But there was no one to kill. At least, nothing human. But yet her pointing continued, straight into the sink. So I peered over the edge, and there he was.

It was clearly menacing, mean, ruthless, evil, sinful, wicked and deserved to die.

Oh, who am I kidding? In fact, it was none of the above.

It was a spider, small, black and about the size of a piece of navel lint. And so tiny and light you could have mailed him and eighty of his friends with a single first-class stamp.

Oh, yes, and deaf. Stone cold permanently deaf. I do not know if spiders are capable of hearing to begin with, but even if they are, this one was now deaf. Because no ears that tiny could have withstood Sarah's high-decibel output and remained functional. I doubt he felt a thing, his ears probably blew out on her first eruption. Heck, even mine hurt, so his must be toast.

His offense was not great, as crimes go. All he was trying to do was go about the business of being a spider, unaware that he's landed in the home of Superwoman, and he is her Kryptonite.

I, myself, did not hate him for being a spider. I wished him no particular ill will. All he wanted in this life was to spin webs, catch flies and make more spiders. I personally do not begrudge any living creature who's diet consists of insects. If that's all the system allows you to eat, I feel you've already been punished enough.

But still, there could be no question. He had to die.

His end was swift. A tissue pierced the air, the swoop, and the deed was done. I've done it thousands of times by now. And every time I feel I should put on an executioner's hood first, purely out of respect. In a just world, he would get full military honors, a twenty-one gun salute and a tomb in Arlington. But the world is often unjust, so I merely hummed "Taps" at toiletside.

New husbands should know that the deed must be done quickly. I do it to protect my wife, because I love her infinitely more than the spider, and she needs protection. Not from the spider, but from herself. For if the spider continues to live and crawl in her sight, she will keep screaming, her veins will further enlarge, her face will further redden, and her eyes will further bulge to life-threatening proportions. (That is where the phrase "bug-eyed" comes from.) So the life of the spider must be sacrificed in order to save the life of my wife.

There are insects I can capture and set free outdoors, but this is not an option with a spider, because Sarah will know that he's right out there on the other side of the wall, and just knowing that he's out there, looking for a way back in, will paralyze her. She can only rest if he is put to rest.

Part of my motivation, I confess, is selfish, because my sole goal is to stop the screaming as quickly as possible. I am convinced that listening to "The Spider Scream," which is its full name, shortens my life. I figure each scream costs me about three days off the end of my life, so every ten screams cost me another month I could spend bouncing grandchildren on my knee.

Each wife's Spider Scream is unique. Sarah's goes something like:

"Yaaaa – WAAAAAAAAAAAAAHH!!!"

Note Sarah's Spider Scream is in two parts, with an inhaled breath in between. That's because the first part, the "Yaaaa," is blurted the very instant the spider is spotted, with no time for inhaling, and so is done with whatever amount of air is in her lungs at that exact moment. This part of the scream is simply the best she can do in the split-nanosecond she has between identification and the need to alert the world.

Then, lungs now empty, she sucks in a fast, huge burst of air and gives the occasion the true blood-curdling siren it deserves, the second half of her war cry:

"WAAAAAAAAAAAAAAAHH!!!"

So the full Monty is:

Yaaaa – WAAAAAAAAAAAAHH!!!"

Today, after years of marriage, I know Sarah's two-staged Spider Scream as well as my favorite high school oldies, and I no longer panic and run for a kitchen knife. I get up from my chair, find the nearest tissue, and head in the direction of the commotion. The football game can wait, Sarah cannot.

I heard on the Animal Channel that there are over 2 million spiders per acre of land, and that a human is seldom more than 10 feet away from the nearest spider. I'm probably going to cancel the cable.

Women Know Pain

Living with Sarah taught me that women tolerate and endure more pain in a year than I shall know in a lifetime.

And that's without even discussing childbirth, which I'm not going to do, simply because it's already been done to death. Every writer, journalist, novelist, editorialist, commentator and humorist on the subject of men and women from the beginning of time has talked about the ultimate pain that women endure bringing life into the world, and how men couldn't handle it.

Besides, no one could explain labor pain better or more directly than the immortal Carol Burnett, when she said, "If men want to understand the experience of childbirth, try this little exercise. First, men, take your upper lip and see if you can touch it to the bottom of your nose. Can you do it? You can? Good. Now take your upper lip and pull it completely over your head." So there it is. Men can understand the birth experience only if they're willing to wear their upper lip like a parka hood.

So that's no contest, and women would clearly win the pain tolerance competition on the basis of childbirth alone. But what amazed me most about life with a wife was to discover that women would still win by a mile even without any points whatsoever for maternity. Labor may represent their crowning achievement in the pain Olympics, but they'd still win medals just for everyday life.

Some female pain, such as monthly cramps, is mandatory, meaning it comes with the territory, it's part of being a woman, unavoidable dues paid for club membership. Other pains, such as labor, childbirth and the decision whether to do so naturally or with anesthesia, are semi-optional. Some women choose to go through it, others do not, but most women make conscious decisions in advance about whether to do it.

But – and this was utterly astounding to me – by far the greatest quantity of excruciating pain suffered by millions of women is completely voluntary!

That's right, most womens' pains are ones they bring on themselves, openly, knowingly, fully aware of what they're doing and that it's going to hurt – and hurt a lot. And while these self-inflicted miseries may be less than that of childbirth in terms of intensity, they exceed labor pain thousands of times over in number. Because while labor only happens to the average woman a small handful of times, most women grit their teeth and laugh in the face of considerable suffering several times every week for much of their adult lives.

Consider all the optional agony women choose to endure just to look more beautiful. Things like ear and skin piercings, breast implants, breast reductions, laser hair removal, hair pulling and stretching devices, eyebrow plucking and bikini waxing, which is nothing more sophisticated than prison camp rip-and-tear torture. (I'm sure if I they used it on me, I'd tell every secret I knew and even some I didn't.) Fellas, remember when you were a kid how you had to steel yourself when Mom had to take off one lousy bandage from your sissy arm, and she told you to clench you teeth while she ripped it off real quick? And even with all that prep, it was so bad you never forgot it? In fact, you still remember it today like it was yesterday? Well lots of women do that every single day, some several times a day. In fact, have you ever seen a woman who looks like she's got a forced smile permanently painted on? It's not painted, her face just finally froze that way after years of gritting her teeth.

One day I made the mistake of asking my wife what the noisy device was that she was using on her legs, and she introduced me to her Epi-Lady. For most men who have never seen one up close, let me explain that the design of an Epi-Lady seems modern enough to the naked eye, but the operating principles behind it are right out of the Middle Ages. Because at its core, the Epi-Lady is a curled coil of wire which vibrates at high speed, traps hair in its coils, and rips them out at their roots with all the delicacy a bear extends to a salmon.

But I had no way to appreciate the high pain threshold required to operate an Epi-Lady on oneself, because my iron-willed Amazon bride showed no outward evidence of trauma – or even discomfort – while using it. She just ran it over her skin again and again, so I assumed it was no big deal. So much so that I asked her if she might use it on a patch of hair on my back I wanted gone. She said, "Sure," and I bared my back. She had used it on me for all of about four seconds before I gently whispered, "YEEEEEEIIIAIAIAIAOOOOOOOAAAAA!!!!" I ran from the room like a baby fleeing the boogieman and threatened to report her to Husband Protective Services. She's agreed to use it in the future only when I'm out of the house. Counseling has helped with the nightmares.

But that's only a fraction of the torment women willingly welcome. There's also the pain of squeezing their feet into shoes that are too small, jamming their hips into jeans that are too tight, skin peels, abrasion treatments, exfoliation regimens, skin detoxifications, vein procedures, and slicing-and-dicing surgeries to remove or redistribute weight elsewhere, and which require a month in isolation and agony to recover. Not to mention spinning classes that burn the thighs, Pilates instruction which bends the body in ways nature never intended, and underwire and Miracle Bras that bunch for cleavage and elevate to the point they block lines of sight.

Shoes make up an entire class of hurt all their own. Not only do women willingly re-conform their feet by cramming them into vessels not shaped like feet – Have you ever met someone whose bare foot comes to a razor-sharp stiletto point? – but they walk on heels that contort their ankles and calves into unnatural alignments. Painful? Of course, but apparently some early caveman was aroused by a cavebabe ambling by on the balls of her feet millions of years ago and women have been suffering through it ever since.

Fellas, if you want to appreciate what it would be like to wear just a modest high heel, try this. Pick out your favorite comfortable walking shoes, but just before you slip them on, stuff one rolled-up wool sock into the back of each shoe so one is crammed under each heel. Then take twenty minutes and walk around the block twice, carry the trash to the curb and make five round trips to the basement. Oh, yes, and take the rest of the night off with your legs in a whirlpool, a bottle of Tylenol and your favorite crying towel. Take it slow this weekend and you should be good by Monday.

My Sarah is so accustomed to pain that she even does it to herself when she draws a bath. I maintain that she does not even need soap, because no living thing, germ or otherwise, could possibly live at the water temperature she uses. I don't have to run the furnace or shovel snow on a winter day if she will just take a long bath, because the heat radiating from the tub is enough to warm the whole house and clear the walks. Sometimes when she gets out of the tub she'll ask if I want to use the water for my bath. If I say yes, I must wait at least an hour before sticking my toe in, and even then I have to go in slowly, testing all the way, adding cold water every time.

How can she stand it? Because she's a woman, and while pain may not be her friend, it is a constant companion and a foe with which she is familiar. Between them they have worked out a mutual respect and a daily working relationship.

So women take it philosophically, embrace discomfort when it serves a worthwhile purpose, and endure shoes which are a pain in the feet, Epi-Lady's which are a pain in the legs, and husbands which are a pain in the . . . . .

Chapter 12

Women Are Artists

Marriage taught me that most women have the soul of an artist. It is certainly true in spades for Sarah.

This is not to say that she and her friends spend time in a studio creating oils and sculptures for a gallery. But they are nonetheless constant Picassos in their daily lives.

While they have no formal easel and canvas, they have a driving inner need to compose, decorate, accessorize and express. Their canvas is their face, hair, nails, body and home.

A woman can see her hair as it could be. She can see a room as it could be. She can see a yard as it could be. She can see her husband as he could be.

Whereever they roam in the world, whether it be one mile from home or ten thousand, they are always scouting for new "colors" with which to adorn themselves and their surroundings, always seeking new heights of composition and expression.

"Colors" can be found literally anywhere. In stores ranging from Bloomingdale's to Bargain Bin, Tiffany's to Target, Gucci to The

Gap, Dayton's to The Dollar Store, and even military installations like Old Navy and The Salvation Army. Other venues might include Home Depot, Pier One, the porch store at Cracker Barrel or a streetside souvenir stand downwind from a slaughterhouse. It could be on Rodeo Drive or on a drive past a rodeo. Any place, any time could be the right time to find that next perfect brush stroke to finish off the Sistine Chapel of her life's work of art. It's a dominant female force of life, and Martha Stewart's career depends upon it.

Men, on the other hand, are more focused on practicality and functionality than on artistic and aesthetic elevation. Take the example of checks for the family checkbook. Men do not see the value of pretty checks. How, men ask, can a serene setting on a check possibly ease the pain of writing an obscenely large payment to the cable company upon its surface? It may be a lovely setting, but it's still a criminal act, and therefore ugly. It's still sucking hard-earned money out of his bank account, and no amount of peaceful serenity will make it less of a violation.

Furthermore, men do not care if the artwork on stamps or paper money ever, ever, ever, ever, ever, ever changes. To a man, the purpose of a stamp is to get the payment to the cable company, not to take someone's breath away en route. When I ask to buy a book of stamps at the postal counter and the clerk asks me what kind of stamp, I always wonder why there is more than one kind of stamp in the first place. Why would anyone want or need more than one form of stamp? The cable bill never changes. So why should the stamp I pay it with ever change? (The Budweiser can hasn't changed in over 50 years, and men love it that way. OK maybe it has, but men didn't notice.)

But I have seen a woman stand dead still at the postal counter for five minutes trying to decide which of the dozens of stamp options best reflects her mood that day. And something about putting a forefinger to her lips seems to help her deliberate, as she ponders, "Fawns or finches? Doves or deer? Lions and tigers and bears, oh my!"

Sure, one could become frustrated with the lady at the counter, start tapping one's foot, let out an impatient "Harrumph." Instead, I choose to view it as an example of the basic goodness of women. For some reason no man can understand, she cares what the bill envelope looks like when she drops it in the slot. But even more remarkable, she cares about the artistic happiness of the party to whom it is addressed. She not only wants to feel good about sending it, she wants the recipient to get a mental boost upon receiving it. She wants someone's mail-receiving experience to be enriched because of a well-chosen chipmunk stamp.

That makes her better than me. She actually cares about the cable company. Incredible! I, on the other hand, do not. Nor can I make myself, even though I've tried. Because my cable goes out twice a month, but if I try to use that fact not to pay the bill, they will see to it that my cable goes out permanently. At times, I have despised the cable company, and wished I could pay the bill with a stamp containing a delicate photo of my raised middle finger. But not Sarah. She wants to share with an anonymous cable company mailroom employee her love of chipmunks, and hopes it brings them a smile. She wants her life to be pretty, and she wants their life to be pretty as well. I shall never be that fine a person, but I'm grateful she is there to set a good example.

Women's artistic drive extends to intricate corners of our lives most men don't even know exist. Like the shade of that little blank tissue sheet that goes inside the envelope with a wedding invitation. Women believe the tissue must be the right color. Men believe the tissue must be a mistake.

Men and women also react differently at the moment they first see an interesting object of art. Men see only the price and immediately calculate a pain-of-purchase reading. Women, on the other hand, instantly teleport the object literally around the world to decide where this item would do the most aesthetic good, be that in their home or someone else's. Sometimes Sarah buys the little gnome because it would look nice on our nightstand, but other times she gets it because, "It's perfect for Becky's sunroom." Sometimes Becky was shopping right alongside us and didn't even know it. Either way, the gnome goes home with us. The other gnomes weep and wave a final good-bye. Becky's sunroom is too small for an extended gnome family.

Men could at least follow along if women would use proper terminology for home decorations. I found out early in my marriage that "throw pillows" are not for throwing, not even for lightly tossing, seldom for so much as touching and never for sleeping on. Another time Sarah came home with what she explained was "an occasional table." I naturally wondered what an occasional table might be the rest of the time. I've kept my eye on it for fifteen years, and it's always been a table. I don't have the heart to tell her, but the store must have given her a permanent table by mistake.

One thing I can say, life is never dull while your artist wife's creative juices run wild, and her reach will extend to the very ends of the earth. Our house has tile from Italy, Japanese porcelain, Irish linens, Spanish furniture, bookends from Greece, Mexican maracas, Hawaiian placemats, Sumatran jungle masks, Tahitian yard torches, Dutch candlesticks and one highly overpriced Colombian emerald. I thought I married a simple small-town girl, but she turned into Marco Polo, converting our house into the design arm of the United Nations. Have we been to all these places? Certainly not. But Pier One seems to have been, and brought back these strange things in their excess luggage space.

Honestly, I have to thank Sarah for exposing me to this international diversity. Left to my own devices, the only connection my or any average man's house would have beyond our own country's borders would be French fries, Danish pastry and German potato salad. Some things, even to a man, are worth crossing an ocean.

Chapter 13

Mall Mission Impossible
The Depth Of
The Female Mind
(Fellas, We're In Over Our Heads!)

Shopping has to hold the ultimate proof of the superiority of the female mind. That proof is in the form of the truly staggering list of choices which women mentally catalog and process every day, compared to the paltry few men manage.

In computer terms, fellas, they have a bigger hard drive than we do. Women have the ability to store more data than men, hands down. It's a talent I envy, and I would gladly buy the upgrade if it were only that simple. But I'm a cave drawing next to the Pentium chip that runs in Sarah's brain, and most of my fellow men are, too. I truly believe the average woman has to make more decisions before eight in the morning than the average man has to make all day.

But, new husbands, to fully prepare yourself for this next stage in your marital education, you must first learn the ritual of hitting the mall together. And that demands that you master the Shopping Dance, which differs from all other dances in one major regard – the woman leads.

Yes, the Shopping Dance is a formation performed with the woman in front, and her husband a respectful few feet behind and several degrees to one side, and from there it's simple: JUST FOLLOW HER AROUND. Don't lose sight of her, don't let the gap between you grow too wide, and try not to rear-end her when she stops. And as you perform your supporting role in this serpentine Shopping Dance, as she winds her way through a maze of racks and bins, continue to repeat the mantra: "No, I'm right here, honey. Right behind you. I got your flank. I'm your wingman, sweetheart. Blue Light Leader, you are free to browse, free to browse, no bogies in sight. Repeat, this is a target-rich environment, show no mercy, charge at will and take no prisoners."

Once you have mastered the Shopping Dance, men, try to open your eyes to the truly awesome vastness of the world these women command. I hope it's true that men and women are equally intelligent – all studies say they are. But, gentlemen, women must be using more of their brains than we are, because they keep track of so much more information than we do.

Case in point – shoes. On the surface, it sounds simple. After all, how complicated can basic footwear be? And men's shoes, it's true, are basic. In fact, they're called simply "shoes." Just "shoes." Regardless of style or cut or function, if it goes at the end of a man's leg, it has but one name – it's a "shoe." They're all, all, all just "shoes." What an uncomplicated world men live in.

Women, on the other hand, don't have a single pair of anything generically known as "shoes." They have subcategories and subspecies for every change in footwear. Women have pumps. And clogs and flats and slings. Heels and open-toed. Mules and spikes, flip-flops and strappy sandals. Scrunchy boots, stilettos, wedges and T-straps. Men don't know what any of these are. It's a code they use to keep us out of the conversation. A man doesn't know a pump from a flat. All a man knows is, "When ya got a flat, you need a pump!"

And the number of colors women memorize is nothing short of incredible. How is it that women know every name for every color ever invented? It's an endless list, but for women, apparently no big problem.

Every woman in the world knows, for example, what color periwinkle is. Most women wouldn't have to think twice, it's that deeply ingrained. But there aren't a hundred men in the universe who could identify periwinkle. Because men only know the eight colors in the big fat crayon box from first grade. In fact, we've forgotten about six of those; most of us are pretty well down to black and brown that we can understand.

But women know every color, tint, shade, pastel, variation and gradation of hue. Sarah's shoe catalog – what a mind-boggling collection of complexity. Exotic names I had never seen before. Aspen, mauve, ecru, taupe. Seabreeze, eggshell, crimson, indigo. Khaki, beige, honeysuckle, ivory, lavender, sandstone, heather, mist, teal, satin, flax, coral, cream, nugget, pearl, saddle, daisy, black, ebony, charcoal, raven, midnight, parsley, persimmon, pineapple, periwinkle, papaya, peach, purple, pink, poppy, pixie, powder, pewter, peapod, pansy, pumpkin, puce, pomegranate, peppermint, pancake, pumpernickel, champagne . . . (whew!) . . . and toast.

On the other hand, men's shoes? Black and brown. And sadly, tragically, for men, one choice too many. Because he still has to turn to his wife and say, "Honey, which one should I wear tonight? Huh? I got black and brown here, and . . . please, help me out, make a call? This'll bust a guy's brain. How do you do it?"

For the true depth of female color intricacy, nothing in my experience tops what a woman said to me one night after a standup show. Having heard me reel off that long list of shoe colors, this gentle woman tracked me down and said while that may have been impressive, "You forgot seafoam." She was right. And I was floored. And to any man not frightened by that level of intellect, let me say, and with respect, you are a fool. This woman listened to a rapid-fire list of over 50 colors, and when it was over, she knew both which ones had been said and which had not. Any woman who can do that, I'm afraid of, and my fellow men should be, too.

But it doesn't stop there. Ever shop for makeup with a woman? There are over 4,000 different makeup products in a WalMart alone. And women know every single one. Not that she uses them all – of course not. From the thousands, she has carefully selected 15 to 20 that make up the travelling squad. But she's aware of them all.

By contrast, men have two makeup options: shave, and don't shave. Not that women don't envy men here. Most women think it'd be great to have it as easy as a man, just to be able to wake up on a Saturday morning, hop right out of bed, look in the mirror and say, "I look great. Let's get outta here. C'mon, honey, we're burnin' daylight."

But most women can't do that, so have a little sympathy, men.

Most women have to get up in the morning, confront the mirror, and start mixing chemicals. And there are so many of them that they really need to know what they're doing. Because they've got eyeliner, lipliner, browliner, lidliner, blush, rouge, foundation, oily creams, non-oily creams, cold cream, wrinkle cream, face cream, hand cream, foot cream, day cream, night cream, creme rinse, mascara, lip shadow, lip gloss, lipstick. More colors than a New England autumn, more flavors than a Vegas buffet.

Women actually have – are you ready for this? – moisturizer and dehydrator. Let that sink in. Moisturizer AND dehydrator. Apparently part of their body is a desert, and another part is a swamp. And it takes a serious land-management effort to keep it all in balance.

And the intricacy of women's nails. There are over 1,500 different products because women have nails. Some to cut, shape, sharpen and hone; others to strengthen and fortify; others to decorate and adorn; and just in case everything fails, they'll get fake ones and glue those puppies on. And they'll do it, too, because nails are simply that important. Nails serve a lot of important functions for women. They can be used offensively, defensively, erotically, for ripping or tearing, for bragging to other women, or to lure men.

On the other hand, in a man's world, nails have but two purposes: beer tabs and nose picking. It's sad to admit, but boogers-to-Budweiser pretty well sums men up. A simple world for simple beasts.

Chapter 14

Kiss Food As You Know It Good-Bye

A well-matched husband and wife become such a good team that they are at times interchangeable. One may even sense the needs of the other through unspoken communication and respond immediately and instinctively. When speaking of such a couple, there are even certain sentences into which you could drop either the word "husband" or "wife" and the meaning would be the same.

However, there is one sentence into which only the word "wife" will fit, and "husband" just will not do.

Virtually no one has ever uttered these words:

"My husband has us on this crazy diet!"

Husbands do not suddenly shake up and reprogram a family's basic dietary routine. Husbands do not read food articles in Good Housekeeping. Husbands do not listen to the latest Oprah or Today Show story on cutting-edge nutrition. Husbands do not worry about toxins around every corner. Husbands are not, in fact, intellectually curious about any quality of the food they eat other than whether it's mouthwateringly delicious. Husbands want to know only if it tastes good. If so, eat it. If not, beat it.

Husbands did not make Dr. Atkins a multimillionaire. If Dr. Atkins had to rely on husbands for an income, he'd be on food stamps instead of on his yacht.

Husbands don't care about counting carbs. Husbands are more interested in counting cards. At a Vegas blackjack table. After a steak dinner. A 44-ounce sirloin. Potato with double sour cream and butter. Apple pie with cheese and ice cream. Any concession to calorie counting? Of course. Six lite beers.

No, only wives derail years of perfectly blissful eating habits and embark the both of you on journeys into uncharted taste wastelands. So beware, my fellow chowhounds. Their antennas are always up for the latest food fad passing in the wind, and there's no predicting who they might listen to. Wait, that's not right. They listen to everybody. They're curious about every new food theory, credible or not, credentialed or not, tasty, satisfying and filling or not. And if that weren't bad enough, they're willing and eager to try out every single new food theory . . . on you.

You like meat, don't you, you savage, drooling carnivore? Big juicy T-bones, cheese-smothered burgers, bacon-wrapped filets. Well get 'em while they're hot. And get 'em while you're single.

Because your mad-scientist wife reads, watches and listens to every trendy new idea about what to eat, and you're the rat in her lab. It may not happen during the first week, maybe not even the first year or the first ten. But somewhere in your future there will come a day when she will announce that food as you know it has come to an end.

She may tell you straight up that the family needs to eat better and some changes are coming. But your first warning might be more subtle, as when you walk into the kitchen and notice that something you can't quite put your finger on is different.

Then it hits you. "Hey, where are the Doritos? There are always Doritos on this counter, but they're gone." So you check the fridge. "Wait a minute. Where's the summer sausage that was here? It was behind the nacho cheese yesterday, plain as day, almost a whole log. Speaking of which, where's the nacho cheese? And where'd all this fruit come from? Wait, what's this new gizmo next to the sink? A Hydro-Juice-Master 3000? And what the hell do we need with Gentle Ben's Seven-Grain Bread? Who even knew there were seven grains?"

Poor guy. No one warned you, didn't send you a letter or a memo, not even a Post-It note on your dresser, as would have been polite. You didn't even get one last farewell savory meal before the curtain fell. It just happened, a fait accompli, and now your find yourself thrust unwillingly into . . . The Health Food Zone.

Few husbands ever go willingly into The Zone, for two main reasons – it's not filling, and it tastes lousy. To a man, eating things that taste bad and don't satisfy violates the entire purpose of eating as he knows it. But wives factor other considerations into the equation – frivolous things like nutrition, health, balance, regularity, blood pressure, cholesterol and longevity – and open their minds to new diet regimens certain to disrupt the taste buds of the men who married them. Men who wooed their wives over beef and pizza and now strain in vain to find satisfaction with hummus, artichokes and polenta.

The first phase is when she presents you with a new replacement snack. Instead of the Snickers Bar you're used to and crave, she'll hand you your first rice cake. She hopes you'll fall for it because, after all, it's called "cake." But be warned in advance, a rice cake is not "cake" in any true sense of the word. Real "cake" contains eggs, butter, sugar, flour, artificial color and lots of gooey sour cream icing. A rice cake, however, contains nothing the male palate wants. It consists of spun rice, shot full of air, sprinkled with sand, held together with school paste, and it's every bit as appetizing as opening your mouth in the middle of a dust storm. The only cake it resembles is the deodorant cake at the bottom of a public urinal. Only a rice cake is less tasty. (Don't ask how I know. I was drunk.)

But you love her, and marriage is supposed to be about trust, right? So you bite into on your first rice cake and you start to chew. At least that's what it feels like you're doing. You could almost swear that your teeth are moving in their old up-and-down motion, doing that grinding thing they've been doing ever since they emerged through the surface of your gums as a tot. But something's missing from the normal experience. A piece has dropped out of the equation, the whole is incomplete. What is it, you ask. Hmmm. Let's see. Wait! That's it. At last, you know the missing ingredient which makes this different from every other meal you've ever eaten.

FLAVOR.

This is one of the most mystifying scientific achievements any husband ever encountered. He knows he's chewing something, he can feel it on his lips and gums. Everything's working as it should from his end. But in all his years of chewing and swallowing, the activity has always produced taste sensations, both good and bad, but so consistently that he thought it was an unavoidable byproduct of the process. But somehow, the new husband learns, to his horror, the rice cake people have discovered how to avoid it. Because he's chewing and chewing and chewing and chewing and chewing, but his taste buds are completely comatose. Nothing is ringing their bell, waking them from peaceful slumber. He is, in effect, chewing crunchy air. In that regard, eating a rice cake is a little like living in Los Angeles.

What other alien dining sensations will the unsuspecting new husband learn from his wife? For one, few single men ever sample sprouts. But nearly all married men have recoiled at the sight of a small bird's nest on one corner of their dinner plate, and asked whether they're really expected to eat this. For the uninitiated, sprouts are tubular, nearly-transparent and look like the ideal material out of which to make packing material, insulation or pet bedding. In short, they look right at home in just about any factory or national park, but not on your plate next to the potatoes.

Sprouts are what mankind ate before the invention of the spear. Without the spear, meat was out of the question, so man had to eat what he could catch with his hands, mainly sprouts and a few of its leafy cousins.

But once the Iron Age arrived with its spears, knives and arrow tips, man nurtured and developed his inner T-Rex, and sprouts settled into its their rightful place as rabbit food. Sadly, many

95

wives today hate rabbits, and constantly steal their food for human consumption. One day the American Congress of Rabbits will revolt and reclaim all sprouts, but until that glorious day, new husbands will have to seek out high-fat cheese and bacon-based salad dressings with which to drown sprouts and make them edible.

And she'll teach you about tofu. Years ago you could see tofu coming and steer clear. It just came in one form, sort of like white custard, so if it wasn't your cup of curd, you could eat around it. No longer, because today scientists working for Kraft and Dow Chemical have found ways to disguise tofu as hot dogs, salami, bologna, chicken, pork, beans, soup, pasta, cheese, chili, pepperoni, chips, pizza and ice cream. All of which enables the cunning wife to more easily slip multiple forms of soy into her husband's diet without proper disclosures, waivers and releases being signed.

She'll teach you the glory of eight glasses of water per day. (Which will be in keeping with your rice cake experience, because water is the only substance equally as tasteless as a rice cake.) Be advised that once she starts making you drink eight glasses of water a day, ostensibly in an effort to improve your health and help you live longer, to the contrary, your life just got shorter. And that's because that much water running through the body every day is time-consuming. It not only takes more time to drink that much more water, it takes up more time to get rid of that much more water.

On average, eight glasses of water a day will consume one extra hour of your time every day, divided evenly between finding, pouring and drinking water, finding and using restrooms, and washing up. That's 365 hours of your year that are now gone, no longer available for other pursuits. If you have 50 years left on this earth, that's 760 days of your remaining life dedicated to drinking and peeing, which is over 2 years. Congratulations, you no longer have 50 years, you have 48. OK, you technically still have 50, but time spent drinking water and going to the toilet does not count on any male quality-of-life scale.

Don't believe me? Ask any man what he would do if he was asked to choose between (A) another 50 years of happy, fun life, or (B) another 1,000 years of life but 950 of those years have to be spent drinking water and urinating. No man would choose to live another 1,000 years if he had to spend 95% of that time as a Roman fountain.

And she'll teach you about oxidants. But don't be afraid, it's not the same as oxidation. It just means you're going to eat more tomatoes, not that you're going to rust.

And she'll teach you about salad. Garden, Caesar, Cobb, Waldorf, tossed, pasta, Greek, cucumber, lettuce, spring, summer, fall, noodle, radish, spinach, potato, seaweed, watercress, egg and endive. Nearly every green, red or yellow thing that grows anywhere on this earth will be staring back at you from your salad bowl, so be ready.

Leafy things you never heard of before will suddenly appear on the end of your fork. Arugula will be there. It won't help to protest that "arugula" sounds like you're clearing your throat, it's now part of your diet, so bite down and get used to it. You will find to your surprise that "kale" is not a NASCAR driver, but part of your dinner. You'll also be expected to eat a leek. (No, it's not what you think, you'll live.) And wait till you try cilantro, which no matter how much it's washed still tastes like the soil it was pried from. If you'd like to sample cilantro but don't have any in the house, just lick the lint filter from your clothes dryer. For my money, I've always thought "cilantro" would have been a far better name for the kid on "I Love Lucy" than Little Ricky. Cilantro Ricardo would have been a name for the ages. No man wants to be "Little" anything.

But what wives teach husbands about in spades is FIBER.

New husbands seldom bring to the marriage any prior knowledge of fiber. But they soon learn that while fiber may not make the world go round, fiber does make the world go Number Two. And a new wife's sponge-like brain eventually masters the fiber content of everything and her internal calculator tracks his daily intake meticulously to ensure that his diet contains 150% of the fiber necessary to keep regular an adult bengal tiger.

Before long, the new husband find himself eating gritty, grainy substances he once thought were meant only to be sprinkled on slippery winter driveways for better traction. Granola, oat bran, wheat germ, flax seed, rye, caraway, sesame seed, whole grain flour and sun-dried prunes.

Apparently the key to long life is not over-exerting one's bowels. So she doesn't want you to strain when you poop. But she'll take it to the point that you no longer have any say over when you poop. You are truly an accident waiting to happen, and would be best advised to walk around with a bucket in one hand. And when you must stop to use it in the middle of the mall, and passing fellow husbands look at you curiously, just say, "Fiber

One." They'll leave you alone. They've been there, and they'll keep walking, buckets in hand.

The Key To Marriage?
It's The Economy, Stupid!

Love makes the world go round.

Love is a many splendered thing.

Love will keep us together.

Our love is here to stay.

Love is in the air.

All you need is love.

Love conquers all.

We can live on love.

OK, HOLD IT! I was with you for a while, it sounded warm and sentimental, I could almost hear the Kenny G album. But those last three? Now you're getting officially carried away.

A married couple can live on love, which always solves everything, and that's all they need? What were you smoking when you wrote that, and do you have any left over?

A married couple can live on love only if (1) they reside in a parent's basement, or (2) one of them has a trust fund. But for everyone else, an essential element of marriage is money, as in the sentence, "Why is there never enough money?"

All other married couples must learn how to earn and budget, budget and earn, while still keeping love alive. For some, love, it turns out, is quite fragile, and can become endangered when accompanied by the strain of poverty and repeated calls from the electric company. Seems it's hard to drive to the opera in a car that's been repossessed.

So a new wife must teach her husband the rules of money. Not every household is the same, but here are the important lessons Sarah has taught me:

1. Money left out in the open may disappear.

You come home tired, anxious just to sit down with the paper or TV and treat yourself to some much-deserved relaxation. As you come through the door, your hands shoot through your pockets and you unload the contents – keys, pen, mints and cash – on the kitchen counter. An hour later, you rise from the sofa and stroll back through the kitchen. And there they are, just as you left them – keys, pen and mints. Wait. "Hey, where's my cash?"

Good question, Oh, Impossible-To-Fool-You-Never-Miss-A-Trick-Endlessly-Astute One. But the problem is, it's the wrong question. It's not "your" cash that's missing, at least not by the time it disappeared. Certainly, it was indeed "your" money as you drove home and it was deep in the bottom of your pants pocket, no argument there. But you just couldn't leave well enough alone, could you? No, you had to reach down, grab the wad of bills, and bring them out into the evening air. And once exposed to the outside world, "your" cash started to gradually change its properties. While still in your fingertips, sure, it's still mostly "your" money, though exposing it to a wife's view may put that status in jeopardy. But the instant you released your grip and set the money on the counter, it was no longer "your" money.

It became "our" money.

Now the only way it's ever going to be your money again is if you beat her back to it. But instead, you turned your back on it, voluntarily walked away, left it there in the kitchen open and unguarded. What were you thinking? You don't leave "our" money up for grabs!

Because "our" money can change properties, too, and it's already too late. "Our" money became "her" money when she swooped in like an eagle lasered on a mouse, only quieter and with more grace. Once her talons closed around it, the our money which used to be your money transformed to her money, and the only way you'll ever see it again is to ask her for some of her money, a request she will likely refuse because you've proven yourself once again to be so hopelessly careless with it.

2. Husbands don't get change back.

You're off to the movies and cutting it close for showtime. You, Gallant Husband, stand in line for tickets, and you hand Ms. Elegant Wife a $50 bill to dash in line for popcorn and drinks.

It's a good movie, you laugh, you cry, you crunch and slurp your goodies. You ask yourself why it is that popcorn is free at a bar but at the movies it's more expensive than heroin.

Later, as you both walk to the car in the evening breeze, you inquire as to whether there might have been any change from that $50.

"No, sorry," she replies demurely.

"What?" you recoil with surprise. "I know movie popcorn's expensive, but fifty dollars?"

"No, the treats were only eleven-fifty," she says.

"So where's the rest of it?"

"Gone. Sorry."

"Gone? Gone where? Gone for what?"

Comes the reply, with her sweetest smile and wink:

"Service fee."

3. Money she lends you must be paid back. Money you lend her is gone forever.

All clear? Enough said.

4. Sarah's jewelry is an "investment." A boat for me would be a "luxury."

Before marriage, most men view buying jewels as equivalent to flushing money right down the crapper. Jewels are, after all, rocks. What sane person would pay good money for mere rocks?

But Sarah taught me that's standard old male wrongheadedness. She patiently explained, as I listened enrapt, that money spent on diamonds and other gems isn't money wasted at all. It's an *"investment."* What a relief!

She and her sisters know that men have a weakness for the word "investment." It makes men feel like men to talk investments with other men. It's a word which connotes wisdom, shrewdness, business acumen, worldly savvy, refinement and seasoned maturity. Men want to have as many investments as possible. Men also keep score with investments, revering good investments and mocking bad ones. It feeds their competitive instincts, and makes them feel important and Trump-ish.

The magic of the word "investment" in this setting, women discovered, is that it ups the ante men can be persuaded to pay to buy in to the marital poker game. Whereas a man wouldn't pay more than $10-20 for a mere "rock," suddenly he'll fork over $10,000 for a marquis cut 1.5-carat "investment." (Some men, sadly, are still making payments long after the divorce. Bad investment.)

So for about the last century, women have changed their game plan to one of getting their men to think of jewels as an investment, by emphasizing the argument that certain special rocks hold or increase their value over time, as opposed to the boat he wants, which will be worthless in 15 years. It's a shameless appeal to a man's inner Rockefeller, but males are easily led astray, and it usually works.

The weak point in the female argument is that an "investment" means an asset which will be sold in the future so as to yield the big return which was the purpose of the enormous pile of cash "invested" in the first place. A man usually protests the first time he's told to think of ten grand for a ring as an investment.

"It's not an investment if we're never gonna sell it," he pleads. "Are we ever gonna sell it?"

She's way ahead of you, fella.

"No. But we could, if we had to."

"But we won't, so it's not a investment."

"But we could, so it is."

"But we won't."

"But we could."

"But we won't."

"But we could."

Last one to speak wins. Any man think he can win that one? It's an investment.

5. First person in possession of odd money gets it.

Every family has regular, scheduled, predictable money coming into the house, like salaries and paychecks. Everyone knows the normal bills that money covers, so there's not much argument over who it belongs to.

But then there's the occasional random, odd money which shows up. And the question becomes: Whose money is that? The answer, Sarah taught me, is that it belongs to whoever is lucky enough to be home the day it arrives.

This one I learned when an insurance transaction resulted in a refund we were due of about $500. This is money you know is coming, you just don't know when. All you know is that one of these days it'll show up in the mailbox. Sarah left me this voicemail message to let me know the money had arrived, on her watch:

(Singing) "I'm in the money, I'm in the money. I got the State Farm refund check today, baby, and it's M-I-N-E!!! Hee-hee-hee. Bye."

6. Never buy a luxury item for yourself unless you can afford two.

Hey, fella, what's your weakness? Cars? Motorcycles? Big screen TV's? El primo aged scotch?

How about golf? Let's say you've had your eye on a full set of top-of-the-line golf clubs for as long as you can remember. But they're $2,500 and most of your money is tied up in your latest

Cartier "investment." So you can't buy them today, which would be perfect with the weather so beautiful and all. No, you'll have to be patient and save up some green.

After several months, you might think you're ready. You've got about $2,400 in your special earmarked account, and you can start to feel those new club grips in your fingers. If you were single, no question about it, those clubs would be yours by nightfall.

But you're a married man now, and, as a loving wife will teach you, the rules are different. Now, even though you have enough money for what you want, you don't have enough money.

Not until you double your savings.

Sure, it sounds mysterious, because you've never been through this before. So let me be your guide.

If you were to buy the clubs and take them home, your Better Half , if all went well, might just smile and wish you well. But the clock has started ticking.

Inside 30 days, something new will appear in your house. It could be anything – furniture, carpet, draperies, artwork, crystal centerpiece, necklace. All that can be known for certain is that it will be an item no husband would ever buy for himself, it will cost around $2,500, and it will be accompanied by your charming wife's explanation that, "If we could afford your golf clubs, we can afford my necklace."

This will catch every new husband flatfooted, because it defies everything passing for logic in the male world. "Of course we can't afford the necklace," he'll scream, "because we already bought the golf clubs. In fact, the reason we can't afford the necklace is because we could just barely afford the golf clubs." In MaleSpeak, it's only elementary that money spent on him is no longer available to be spent on her. Money can only be spent once, right?

But she'll shake her head slowly from side to side, calmly, with a smile, the same way one does when returning home to find that the dog has chewed up an old throw pillow. She'll explain such limited thinking misses the point that if we're doing well enough to afford such nice sports equipment, a tiny item like a necklace should be no problem for such an affluent family.

So smile right back at her, Daddy Warbucks, and tell her how nice she looks with that new necklace. Besides, you have at least 30 days to cool off and relax before the bill for the necklace arrives. You learned a valuable lesson, and it only cost $2,500. Fun or luxury items always cost twice what it says on the price tag. There's no such thing as a 2-for-1 sale. In marriage, it's always 1-for-2.

Chapter 16

How Does She Walk So Fast?

I believe my wife has a secret hyper-speed forward gear hidden somewhere in her body that BMW would love to steal. While I've never actually seen her shift into it, I have often seen the results, and they always leave me breathless. As in panting like a St. Bernard.

Because I am almost a foot taller than my wife, and my legs are much longer than hers. I'm in reasonably good shape, no major disabilities, my joints and limbs all within an acceptable range for a gent my age.

But for some possibly supernatural reason, as we walk the world together, I simply cannot keep up with my wife.

How is it possible for a 5'6" woman to beat a 6'3" man into, around, and back out of the mall every time? And the eerie part of it is she does it effortlessly!

Sarah must have a tiny Prius motor inside, because you never hear her accelerate. She turns, she surveys, she focuses, and she hits Han Solo hyperspace. Her feet don't seem to be moving especially fast, she looks like she's barely exerting at all. But she is sailing away on a wind that has eluded my sails, and if I don't take off after her – and how – it'll soon be too late.

Because at her height, she can quickly disappear behind sales counters, department store displays or into the produce section, and once that happens, she's gone, baby, gone. And once she disappears, I am instantly transported back to seven years old and that first time I lost my parents in public. My biggest fear is that a voice will eventually have to be boomed over the intercom, "Would Sarah please report to the service desk. Sarah to the service desk. We have a little lost husband who says he belongs to you. Please hurry, he's crying."

Husbands of lost wives all have the same facial expression as they walk the store in search of their mates. It's sort of a head-bobbing, tip-toeing, furrowed forehead, wide-eyed hundred yard stare, as he tries to look through and around people. Mostly what they're searching for in their mind is to recall what she's wearing today. Being observant is not a husband's strong suit, and even though he just drove to the store right next to her in the car, now that he's lost her he can't quite remember what she has on. In my mind I can already hear the intercom.

How does she do it? How can she be so fast? Does she have little jetpacks in her shoes? How can she glide like a gazelle while I plod and wheeze like Bigfoot? All I know for sure is that it must be genetic, because my tiny mother-in-law would need to buy two more inches just to make it to five feet tall, and she's even faster than her daughter – with two knee replacements!

I used to go on neighborhood walks with them, but no more. It's too humiliating. Their arms pumping, legs churning, smiles beaming, fluid studies in forward motion. While I have to break into an awkward, graceless, huffing trot just to stay in the same zip code.

The news for husbands is not all bad, though. Once you accept the reality that she's faster and quicker, there are many ways to use it to your advantage. Rushing for a place in line at the airport? Relax. Send her ahead to claim a spot, then take your time and save your composure. She's quicker, smaller, can dart around obstacles, and she'll be holding a place for you when you arrive at your leisure. I use Sarah every time we need a place in any line, be it restaurant, movie, taxi, theater, stadium, mall or market. She's not only more speedy and agile, but also more aggressive, and the world just seems to get out of her way in a manner I will never experience.

So need to catch the postman with some outgoing mail? Don't break your leg, send Ms. America Ferrari. She'll be back in the house, mission accomplished, before you even could have found your other shoe. Oh, yes, and a shirt. And pants. You don't want another incident like last time. The postman still looks at you funny.

Chapter 17

Women Have The Right Of Way
Always!

Recall I observed that the world just seems to move out of Sarah's way as she passes through it. That seems to be true for many if not all women, and I find it endlessly fascinating. And I want it. Sarah can stand at one side of a crowded room, and if she wants to walk to the other side, she just does it. And in a straight line. And without breaking stride! How is that possible? What sort of parting-of-the-Red-Sea magnetic forces are at work here?

On the other hand, if I wish to cross the same room, I must bob and weave, start and stop, sidestep, advance, retreat and say "Excuse me" at least 26 times. By the time I make it to the other side, where the bar is, the party's over. How dearly I would love for the world to move out of my way for one day the way it moves out of Sarah's every day.

I think credit or blame goes to our parents, who taught all their young sons that one of the first rules of social interaction is "Ladies First." Here's another truism we're given as kids and accept blindly as part of everyday life. Boys are trained to hold the door, stand aside, get both on and off the elevator last, take the last cab, order your food last, wait your turn, look around, scan the horizon, look for women, see if any nearby are on unfulfilled missions, help them, see them on their way, bid them good day, and then and only then may you enter the emergency room and get that head wound stitched. Boys are also trained to give up their seats to any standing woman on a bus. So while a man may feel relieved to get the last open seat when he gets on, he knows it will only last until the next woman boards. Then he'll have to either give it up and stand, or risk the glaring stares of all women on the bus, whose expressions are saying, "Do you have no manners? Were you raised in a barn? By wolves? Perhaps in a barn by wolves?"

Men have mostly Sir Walter Raleigh to blame for the public rule that politeness be extended to all women. You'll recall he was the first to famously lay his coat over a puddle so that a woman could step across. Some say women have been walking all over men ever since, those "some" being mostly bitter, beaten men.

(Actually, she was more than just "a woman," she was Queen Elizabeth The First. And despite Raleigh's legendary gallant gesture, she was not a good sport when Sir Walter subsequently took up with one of her Maids of Honour. She was, in fact, so little amused that she had him thrown into the Tower of London. Apparently good manners will only buy you just so much goodwill. Beyond that, she'll hit you with whatever is within her powers. So the lesson is don't fool around on royalty. They have a lot of powers, and they can always find an empty cell. Better to fool around, if you must, on less powerful women, like Lorena Bobbitt. What's the worst she could do? On second thought, better not fool around on any of them.)

The point is that once Sir Walter Raleigh set the soggy jacket standard of chivalry, men ever since have been trained to get out of women's way and make their passage as smooth as possible. This in turn encourages some women to walk through a crowd with a purposeful strut of entitlement, emitting waves to all males in her path to clear the way, and eyeball daggers to any man who didn't get the memo. I know. I've clumsily and obliviously been that guy a few times. And woe – and "Whoa!" – was me.

In general, "Ladies First" applies to everything except dying. When it comes to death, women apparently don't want the right of way, and they don't get it. On average, they get eight more years than men. That's eight more birthdays, Christmases, Thanksgivings, Halloweens and Sears Annual Kenmore Days. "The Weaker Sex?" Not if longevity and stamina are part of the definition. And they are.

And why do they live longer? Well, it's just a theory, but my idea is that it's usually the husband who mows the grass in the heat of summer. He also shovels the driveway and hangs outdoor Christmas lights in the middle of winter. He paints the house, prunes trees and cleans out gutters. If someone needs to run out to the car in the middle of a blizzard to warm it up or bring it closer, it's usually him.

She, on the other hand, eats first, sits while he stands, comes in from the cold first, and waits indoors for the car to be brought around. It's elementary why his time would be up first. He just simply wears out. More exposure means more wear and tear means more erosion and a shorter life cycle. After all, even a young kid knows if you're rough on your toys and leave them out in the weather, they don't last as long.

"Man"
The Only Dirty Three-Letter Word

Surely it's not a good sign for males that the phrase "Oh, Man!" means either that (1) something has gone horribly wrong, or (2) major unpleasantness has occurred.

But that's what we keep saying, every time we miss a bus, burn our tongue, stub a toe, drop our eyeglasses overboard, lose our keys, spill an open paint can, bail a child out of jail, rub a blister, rear-end a squad car, chip a tooth, whiff on the first tee, lose a bet or get an audit notice.

That's not a bad example. Let's say you've just pulled an IRS invitation from your mailbox. First words? "Oh, Man!" OK, that's the mild version. If you're given to more earthy means of expression, perhaps "Oh, S#&%!" pops out. Which is even more devastating to we males. Because the message there is that when times are bad, "Oh, Man!" and "Oh, S#&%!" mean the same thing! "Man" and "S#&%" – perfectly interchangeable terms. Say one, say the other, say both. It all means the same thing – "How awful!" Man, Oh Man, Oh Man, Oh Man!

And if such language usage gives men a bad self-image, it starts when we're very young, one or two years old. After all, what were we all taught little girls are made of versus what little boys are made of?

What are little girls made of? Oh, yeah, girls are made of "sugar and spice and everything nice." Really? Everything nice? Every last nice thing on the face of the earth was completely used up in the girl-making process? They used up literally all the nice things making girls? Why those little hogs. They couldn't share at all?

How utterly demoralizing to little boys. "All the nice stuff's gone? Used it all on girls? Whatya got left over for me?"

"Well, I think we can scrape up some snips and snails and puppy dog tails, how's that sound?"

"Great — load me up. What a relief. I was afraid you'd only have junk left over by now. Whew! Thanks for sparing no expense."

Really? That's all we men get? Snips and snails and puppy dog tails? That sounds like stuff that wasn't good enough to go into sausage. Slaughterhouse floor scraps, more like. Perhaps that's the order. Little girls first, then sausage, then little boys, waaaaaay at the bottom.

And the word "Man" itself is used so aggressively in speech. "M" - "A" - "N." It's the root word of so many bad words. Like "MAN-slaughter." "MAN-handle." "MAN-hunt." "MAN-o-war." "MAN-ure!"

No one wants to be "man"-ipulated. Nobody likes to be given a "man"-date. And an automatic transmission is generally preferred and more expensive than a "man"-ual.

Even the first three letters of "male" are "M-A-L", which means "bad." No one wants to be maladjusted, malcontent, malnourished, malodorous, maladroit, have a malady, be malicious or commit malfeasance. OK, maybe you could interest me in a Mal-O-Mar, but that's the only saving grace, and even then I have to be in the right mood.

On a hunch, I conducted a word search to find the most common English phrases containing the words "good man" versus "good woman." The top three "good woman" sayings were all noble and uplifting:

1) "There's nothing you can't do with the love of a good woman."

2) "Behind every successful man, there's a good woman."

3) "I just hope I die in the arms of a good woman."

But on the other hand:

1) "A good man . . . is hard to find."

2) "Where are all the good men?"

3) "There are no good men."

(Of course, there are a few good men, but the Marines claim to have them all.)

While the world has many good men, no doubt, the idea that men are the more evil of the two genders is advanced, at least by inference, every day in the media and elsewhere in our lives.

If you watch or read the news, it can seem as though if anything bad happens in the world, 99% of the time, men did it. Which is not to say all men are bad. But since being good is seldom newsworthy, man after man shows up in the news for the evil he does.

If you knew nothing of the general nature of men and women, and you formed your impression solely from the news, you would assume that men are in charge of the crime, lust, greed, corruption, frauds and scams.

On the other hand, women seem to be in charge of more noble pursuits – the loving and the nurturing, the color, the beauty and the texture of life.

Women Good – Men Bad.

Unfair? Certainly. But it's nonetheless that way in the back of most people's minds. Ask yourself when's the last time there was some serial killer on the loose, some unknown, unidentified serial killer running around wreaking mayhem, leaving a trail of fear, and you said to yourself, "Gee, I hope they catch her. How can ya sleep knowing that mad woman's out there? When will these ladies learn?"

But they always catch him, it's always a man, and I always say to myself, "Geez, that was our team. One of ours. We did it again. When will we learn? We should call a meeting."

And men keep doing it over and over and over at such a rate it would suggest that we may never change. There are currently 2.2 million people imprisoned in the United States, and 96% are male. 2.2 million in prison – and over 2 million are men. Men make up 48% of the country's population, but 96% of the prison population. The conclusion is obvious – women are smarter, and don't get caught as often.

It's even more lopsided on death row – 98.5% men, 1.5% women. It's actually big news when a woman's time is up:

"They're gonna execute another one today."

"So what? What'd this guy do?"

"This one's a woman."

"No way?"

Bonnie and Clyde. Know what made them famous? Here's a hint – it wasn't Clyde. The unique thing about them was that there was a woman at all. Without Bonnie, Clyde would have been just another faceless male bank robber, plenty of 'em to go around, and it's rare they become internationally famous. That's where Clyde was smart – marketing. Because if you can somehow get a woman to help you do anything wicked, you're well on your way to immortality.

And by the way, "Bonnie and Clyde" is the only way we've ever known them. Ever notice which one got her name first?

"Women And Children First!" Got A Problem With That?

I noted earlier the comparison between diamonds as a girl's best friend, while man's is a dog, and I advanced the theory that women came up with the idea. Yes, I believe women thought it up, and here's how. Ready?

They're smarter than us, fellas.

That's what marriage has taught me, I'm truly sorry, gentlemen, and I hope each man finds the strength to go on. But if a man can drop that male ego out of gear for just a minute and look at it rationally, there's little escaping it. Not every battle, not on every front. We men win a few here and there. But many times, on many subjects, they're smarter, they've beaten us, and we might do well to learn a lesson and profit from it rather than continuing to deny the situation.

Not that women usually flaunt it. They don't waste a lot of time bragging. Some women even believe that part of being smarter is pretending not to be smarter – unlike most men, who have to be stroked and praised and reassured all the time. "Oooh, you're the greatest. How do you do it? You're indispensable. What would we ever do without you?" In contrast, it's enough for most women to rule quietly, secure in the knowledge that it's mostly their agenda being followed, their orchestra, playing their melody. You don't have to tell most women they're in charge. They know they're running the place, and they know it in a calm, quiet, secure, confident way.

So I say women thought up the diamond/dog best friend thing because that time they were smarter than men, no contest. Here's another one I guarantee women thought up:

"Women and children first."

To which man can only stand by and say, "Uh, . . . OK. No, I'm glad you said something, honey, I was about to crawl into the lifeboat. D'you believe that? Forgot my assignment, stay here and die! No, you go ahead sweetheart, you're the precious cargo. We'll be all right, OK no we won't, but you go on. Us guys are gonna go to the back of the ship, lock arms and sing 'Kum-Ba-Ya.' See what it's like to be a shark-sicle."

Anybody think that was a man's idea? Couldn't be. Women thought it up, convinced men it was noble, and today we accept it without question. Had it been up to me, if the world had somehow asked me what I thought the rule should be, I would have said "Children first" – sure, let them have their future. After that, I say we should go by upper body strength. If you can kick my tail, you've earned a seat in the boat. But at least work for it and earn it. This is America, right?

But, no, it'll never change, it's too deeply ingrained. It'll always be "Women and children first," and only after that does a different rule kick in – "Every man for himself." Things sure turn primitive once the women and kids are gone.

Think about that. "Women and children first." We learn it so early, practically from birth. It's presumed to be such a basic rule, one we never question, a central part of life itself. And it's not the only one. Women have a better public relations machine working for them than men could ever dream of or pay for.

There are lots of very feminine-friendly phrases that we learn quite young and accept throughout our lives as basic truths:

"It's a woman's prerogative to change her mind."

You have to stand in awe, men. Because that one is simply GENIUS! It's her prerogative to change her mind. Which means if a woman says one thing, but does another, shut up, what's wrong with you, she's entitled, that's her privilege. Of course, if a man does the same thing, he's an a- . . . . . he's a . . . . . well let's just say it rhymes with where you fuel your car. You know, the gashole.

"Hell hath no fury like a woman scorned."

That's a very poetic, intellectual, lyrical, educated way of saying if you get on the wrong side of a woman, you're actually going to wish you were in hell. Hell would be Club Med compared to where you're going to be.

"A woman's work is never done."

Usually because one of her ongoing projects is a man.

You're married now, fella, and only some of what used to pass for English in your life is going to carry over. The married man must learn to say, hear, decipher and interpret many new phrases he seldom, if ever, had to deal with before he stood at the front of a church and, like Columbus, crossed over into the great unknown. Here they are, gentlemen, and like Kevin Costner said in Bull Durham, "Get to know them, they are your friends."

When a young man is about to get married, he imagines that the words he will hear most often are "I love you." They're not. You know what's number one?

"I'll just have some of yours."

Husband: "Honey, I'm gonna get some more barbecue. You want some?"

Wife: "I'll just have some of yours."

Husband: "I was gonna get more lemonade. Any for you?"

Wife: "Hmmmm, I'll just have some of yours."

Husband: (under his breath) "The hell you will. I'll bring you your own plate with your own food on it, but this stuff on this plate is mine!"

Men, here's a little tip. When I get a good bratwurst – and I love a good brat – I instantly load it up with mustard and hot sauce. I don't even personally like mustard and hot sauce, but it keeps Sarah away from it. I call it "Wife Repellent" at my house, and it happens to work. You learn to like it for the privacy.

Sarah has ten words which scare me to death:

"But we were in luck, 'cuz it was on sale."

If finding a sale is the standard by which luck is measured, then I have been very, very lucky in my life. I may be one of the luckiest men alive. Recently Sarah bought a $1200 piece of jewelry, BUT we were in luck, 'cuz it was on sale, and she got it for $600. Which means in her mind, she spent $600, but she saved $600, therefore it was free.

And now we have a second problem. Remember that $600 she saved? What are we gonna spend that on? Life gets complicated when you're as lucky as we are.

There are five words every new husband should look out for because, if your wife says them, she's lying. It doesn't matter that she's the sweetest creature ever to stand in the sunlight, that you're sure she's never told you a lie, and you don't even think she's capable. If she says these five words, do not believe her. Ready? Here they are:

"I....JUST....HOPE....YOU'RE....HAPPY!"

Do not – repeat – do NOT be fooled. It would be fatal mistake to just walk away blissfully thinking, "Great, she's just glad I'm happy." Because those words are actually Wife Code for "Eat dirt and die."

Same thing if she says **"Fine!"**

Be afraid, be very afraid, if she ever says things are "fine."

If you say, "Honey, I'm gonna play cards with the boys tonight" and she says, "Great, have a good time," do you know what that means? It means "Great, have a good time." But if you say "I'm gonna play cards with the boys tonight" and she says "Fine"? Do not – repeat – do NOT be fooled. Because it means "Eat dirt and die," too.

And the third in the She-Really-Means-Quite-The-Opposite trilogy is:

"OK, don't listen to me."

When a wife says this, a husband's ears should perk up and his heart should race like your dog after he's disemboweled your cell phone. "OK, don't listen to me" is what Clint Eastwood would have said in place of "Make my day" if he was Dirty Mary instead of Dirty Harry. It means proceed at your very great peril, and when I'm vindicated I shall never, never, never, never, never let you hear the end of it as long as you live, possibly longer. "OK, don't listen to me" is an incredibly compact shorthand which conveys in only five words that "I've warned you, you're terminally mule-headed and stubborn, you're making a disastrous mistake, I shall prevail in the end, and I shall dance gleefully on your head till the end of all time." Anyone who can pack that large a message into so few words is a force to be respected.

So those are the big three, and it's important for men to know that these red flags mean trouble, because many women won't come right out and tell the men in their lives that they're "mad." For some reason, many women dislike the word "mad" and will never confess to being mad. Sarah hates to admit she's mad as much as the average man hates to admit he's lost. Sarah's never mad. She will, however, enlighten me on the appropriate terminology.

I'm a simple beast, so I'll use simple language and ask, "Why are you mad?"

Comes the hair-splitting reply: "I'm not mad. I'm disappointed. Miffed, aggravated, hurt. Wounded, peeved, annoyed, irked, upset, frustrated, irritated, depressed, anxious, edgy, nervous, tense, bothered, infuriated, angry, incensed, concerned, perturbed, uneasy, troubled, worried, sad, exasperated, apprehensive, discontent, dismayed, disturbed, distressed, displeased, distraught, disconcerted, disillusioned, disgruntled, disgusted, despondent, dejected, let down, unhappy and a little blue, but I am not MAD!"

"That's good news, honey, I was real worried we had a problem there for a second."

Here's a most important phrase every new husband should learn to say:

"So, are you gonna tell me what's wrong or not?"

And you know the answer, fellas? No. She's not going to tell you. Why? Because if you loved her, you'd know!

There are so many new words to learn because now you're married. You might say that's nothing to be afraid of. They're just words, and after all, we live in the land of free speech. Well, let's be honest, not entirely free. Not when you're married. I put the pencil to it, and I calculated that over the course of my marriage, every time Sarah starts a conversation, on average, it costs about 80 bucks. Sometimes more, sometimes less, but at the end of the year, when I totaled it up, it's an average of about $80 every time that sweet love of my life starts talking.

That doesn't mean men need to be afraid of every conversation. Some conversations are free. Like when Sarah says, "Good morning. It's a nice day. Did you sleep well?" No cost at all. However, beware of any conversation which begins with the words:

"I've been thinking."

There's about a kazillion different ways to end that sentence. "I've been thinkin' about the house . . . the yard . . . the patio . . . the entryway . . . the ceiling . . . our vacation" – whatever. All I can say for sure is that if Sarah's been thinkin', it's usually at least a grand. And it often comes with a loan application and monthly payments. Men sometimes get the bum rap that we're uncommunicative. Let's set the record straight. Men have nothing against communication. It's just that some weeks, we're tapped out. "Sorry, honey, payday's Friday, can we talk then?"

Sarah has a magic shorthand sentence she uses to signal that she is immovable and not going to negotiate on a particular subject. She doesn't overuse or abuse it, which makes it all the more powerful when she says:

"Find something about it you like."

Need I say more? Any discussion required? I didn't think so.

And while we're on the subject of language, let me point out that men might not be so commitment-phobic if the terminology weren't so terrifying to the male mind. A simple look at the words we use to describe marriage is enough to send most men running for the nearest monastery:

"Wedlock" – Sounds like prison. If you want men to look forward to being "wed", you should not team it up with "lock", which, let's face it, is not a warm and fuzzy word. No one's ever happy about being locked up, locked down, locked in or locked out. So it should come as no surprise that men are pretty nervous about jumping into "wedlock." You can practically hear the cell door slam. CLANK! "This is the warden speaking, welcome to WEDLOCK. We only have a few rules here at the Big House and they all end with 'Call home first.' Wanna have a drink with the boys? Call home first. Making weekend plans? Call home first. And if you're even thinkin' about writing a check for over twenty bucks, we hope you know the drill by now, call home first."

"Ball & Chain" – Definitely prison. With the added bonus of rusty leg irons, ponderous weight, the clanking of chains and the image of sharing a cell with the Count of Monte Cristo.

"Tie The Knot" – What they do in prison to the rope before they hang you. How comforting!

"Take The Plunge" – What poor unfortunates do off the edge of a pirate ship.

So, women, if you want men to change their attitude toward marriage, start by changing the language. Get rid of references to loss of freedom, pain, isolation, imprisonment, gloom and death. Instead, find a name that combines things important to a man, things like sex, beer, sex, football, sleep and, oh yes, more sex.

Don't call it a marriage. Call it a Lewd-Lager-Eroto-Hail-Mary-Nap-Gasm. Men'll fight each other to get some of that.

All a single man needs to clean anything in his house is a shirt tail and spit. All the elements are there. A little cloth, a little moisture, and dirt doesn't stand a chance. I willingly concede, however, that if the house has more that three bedrooms, he may need a second shirt.

Few men enter marriage with any working knowledge of the Proctor & Gamble cleaning sciences. When I got married, all I had was a moldy sponge, a plastic bucket which originally came full of margarita mix, and a bottle of Mr. Clean so old he still had hair. And I hadn't used any of them in seven years.

And that was enough for any man in singlehood. But once a man lives with a woman, he learns that she operates under different cleanliness parameters. Compared to his Fred Flintstone working in a Bedrock quarry, she's manufacturing microchips in Silicon Valley.

A new husband is no longer allowed to live in filth, and a wife sees filth everywhere. She comes pre-equipped with internal germ radar and she knows the ins and outs of every latest technology to fight it.

So a man must learn from his wife about alien products he's never used and entire sections of the supermarket he's never travelled. What man knew there's one soap for crystal, another for carpet, another for sweaters and another for feet? And what happens if you use the wrong one on the wrong thing? Maybe not much in terms of hygiene, but she'll reclassify you from moron to imbecile and make an urban legend out of you to her friends.

Inside my first month of marriage, Sarah had taught me about hundreds of new products I'd never seen. Most seemed to be designed to make things smell like something they were not. I learned that our table cloth was supposed to smell like a field of clover, our towels like a bed of violets, our kitchen floor like an Alpine forest and our toilet bowl like an April mist. All I previously knew about a bathroom mist was she sure raised a ruckus when I "missed" in the bathroom.

The other odd thing I observed was that while most of the things being cleaned were indoors, the object was to make them smell like they were outdoors. I learned that there was pine this and lemon that and lilac them-over-there. She even introduced me to Orange Glo, which makes everything smell like Florida. Till then, orange glow for me was what I got on my hands when I ate Cheetos.

I learned that there are cleaning products with names like "Joy" and "Cheer" and "Breeze" and "Fantastik" and "Shout" and "Fabuloso" and "Easy Off" and "Scrubbing Bubbles," which "work hard so you don't have tooooooo." With zesty, fun, encouraging names like these, I thought, this can't be so bad. I didn't have a lot of experience with cleaning, other than cleaning out my parents' fridge. But if it was going to be as neato-spiffy-keen as these names implied, I was gonna dig this, because anything both easy and fun is right up my alley.

But every new husband eventually learns the truth, which is that cleaning is not a joy, not full of cheer, never a breeze, and far from fantastik. Neither is it easy, you never shout "Fabuloso," and you, yourself, no one else, just YOU still have to work hard to get things clean. Yes, I'm saying it, Scrubbing Bubbles are little round bald-faced liars. I saw them sing and dance, same as everyone. But now I believe SC Johnson must have had them high on crack to put on that front and sell us such a ridiculous pitch. Even in the 21st century, the only thing which works hard so you don't have to is a maid.

And I haven't even mentioned the most misleading of all – "Endust." By the sound of it, that's a product any man could get behind. What I first thought was, "Wow, think about that. The end . . . of dust! What a great invention. I hate dust, and would love to be rid of it – permanently. I just use this product, and that's the end of dust. In my life. Ever. Sign me up."

So I dusted everything, hating every minute of is, but glad it was the last time I'd ever have to do it. Then I sat back to watch the magic.

As it happens, dust is a prodigiously renewable resource. Apparently it's completely beyond fertile, there is no birth control, and a new herd rumbles into town about every 48 hours. If we could figure out how to run cars on dust, we could tell OPEC to pound sand. You can wipe it away, even throw it away and burn the rag, but replacements are already on the wind. So "Endust" does not really "end dust" in any sense of the words. If there were any truth in advertising, they'd have to call it "Endust For Two Days, Then Dust Be Back."

Likewise, if Endust is a lie, so is "DustBuster." Everyone knows when you really bust someone, you take them off the street. Dust never really gets busted. You can run it in for a few minutes, but it has a great lawyer, always posts bail and is back on the street the second you put down the cloth.

Two cleaning products apparently trying to appeal to men are Kaboom and Easy Off Bam. Men like explosions, so this sounds like fun. But alas, it's another false alarm. Rags and scraping and rubbing and fumes are still part of the equation, and nothing gets blown up except his expectations.

Sarah taught me that some things have to be "pre-treated." This is a fancy word that means some things have to be worked on more than once. As I understand it, pre-treating is the act of sorta-kinda cleaning something before you seriously clean it. In other words, you clean it first so it looks nice for the real cleaning. Most husbands' cleaning efforts are pre-treatments. That's because he gives it a try, but when he does a lousy job, she has to do it again. When Sarah tries to yell at me for a poor effort, I merely claim credit for a successful pre-treatment.

Then I learned there's "deep cleaning." My first reaction was this meant vacuuming while reading Shakespeare. But it really means you must clean not only the dirt you can see, but the dirt under that dirt as well. Marriage taught me that even invisible dirt must be rooted out. Not an easy concept for a man to grasp, because the way men see it, dirt you can't see is the same thing as dirt that's not there. But wives, I learned, are troubled even by invisible dirt. It taunts them and haunts them, and therefore steamers and vibrators must be rented periodically and Saturdays are sacrificed to the sanitary gods. A man is not truly a husband until he's spent the day cleaning something which looked immaculately, perfectly clean in the first place.

And don't even get me started on "2,000 Flushes." If you routinely need 2,000 flushes, you really should see a doctor.

Chapter 22

Wives Are Multi-Tasking Masters

Me and my fellow men seem to be best when we are left alone to do one thing at a time. Men, after all, have the ability to make even a simple chore quite complicated, so any additional distractions could jeopardize everything.

Take watching a football game, for example. Thirty years ago it was simple. You sat, you cheered, you booed, the game was over, and you went on with your life.

But today's man needs a two-hour pregame show to tell him what he's going to see, a three-hour game for him to see it, then a one-hour postgame show to tell him what he just saw. Six total hours for each game, and nothing can be allowed to interfere. With a life this complex, when even a single football game requires this much mental devotion, it's no wonder modern man can only handle one thing at a time, or he will surely lose his place and have to start all over.

But women, particularly wives, are geniuses at multi-tasking. Which is not to say multi-tasking is unique to modern times. My mother was a champion multi-tasker, except she didn't know that was its name. She just called it "trying to do ten things at once." As in, "Will you kids please shut up already, I'm trying to do ten things at once here!? And to think I had you all on purpose."

Mothers in particular are masterful multi-taskers. They can simultaneously fix breakfast, iron a shirt, pour a Jello mold, dress a wound, pay a bill, clip a nail, peel an onion, mend a mitten, set a broken bone, flush a radiator, answer email, disarm a terrorist and still get a 4th grader dressed and polished for class picture day. If I tried to do all that, I'd lose track and peel the terrorist, iron the 4th grader and flush the Jello.

I learned what a multi-tasking whiz my new wife was on our honeymoon. I would have never believed it if I hadn't been there in person, but from the passenger seat of the car she was able to simutaneously read a novel, apply hand cream, talk on the phone, tease her hair, sing with the radio and still retain the capacity to correct my driving. Now that's versatile.

The ball-juggling required just to get a good meal on the table would be enough to stop the average man dead in his single-minded tracks. Try explaining to a man the following parameters for preparing a meal:

The roast will take 5 hours to defrost and 90 minutes to cook.

Mashed potatoes need 5 minutes to peel, 20 minutes in boiling water to cook, and 10 minutes to whip and season.

Gravy mix takes 12 minutes.

Veggies need 16 minutes to steam.

Bread requires 10 minutes to mix, 45 minutes for the dough to raise, and 30 minutes to bake.

Cherry pie needs 45 minutes to prepare crust and filling, 40 minutes to bake, and 2 hours to cool.

Salad prep takes 8 minutes.

Then ask him, given these constraints, what do you have to start when in order to make it all ready at exactly 7 PM? The math alone should be enough to send him into a coma.

For a woman, this is second nature, everyday stuff, no big deal, as easy as learning her ABC's. For a man, this is grade school story problem overload. His eyes will glaze over, roll back in his head, and he'll grab for the only thing that can save him – the phone book.

And he'll make the call. Because the only way he'll ever know to have a full meal come together and be ready at 7 PM is to call Domino's delivery by 6:30. One number, one order, one 30-minute wait, one doorbell rings, and one meal is served. And Mr. One-Job-At-A-Time congratulates himself on another one job well done.

Chapter 23

Women And Their Meetings

I've always suspected and suggested previously that women use "meetings" to secretly take votes and change the rules on the men in their lives. This is because women learned earlier than men that two heads are better than one, three are better than two, and four billion – their worldwide population – is a force that cannot be topped.

Most men are clueless about the elaborate network of meetings women use to carry out their ongoing campaign to stay 1-up, 2-up, and way-way-way-up on their men. That's because most men are isolated, self-contained, alone, foolishly deluded into believing each can handle it all by himself in-house. Men have no support group, no one to call when defeat is approaching and all but inevitable. Put in everyday terms, men won't ask for directions in life, just as they won't ask for directions in the car. It's just too embarrassing.

So while the male world is fragmented and unorganized, the female world pulses and hums like a single giant supercomputer, each woman sharing with any of her sisters what she has learned about taming the savage male beast. That is how they are conquering the world, one broken male will at a time.

When and where do the meetings take place? Any time and any place where two or more women are together and beyond male earshot. What men don't realize is that every female-only conversation lasting over five minutes includes at least one version of "This Is How I Handled My Man When He Did What Your Man Did And Now He Don't Do That No More."

With so many meetings going on in so many places for so many years, one might assume the meeting topics range far and wide, but that is not the case. To the contrary, most could be titled "The Care, Feeding, Training, Discipline and Domestication of the Primitive Adult Male Free-Range Moron Homo Sapien." Which indeed could be the formal name for most daytime talk shows. "Oprah," little-known fact, is actually an acronym for "Outwitting Peristently Rude & Arrogant Husbands."

And because women don't announce their meetings publicly, men don't realize they're taking place. Therefore, men believe that when they run off with their friends for a guys' night out or weekend getaway that the lives of the women they leave behind are merely on hold. Men actually think that when they get away for hunting or golf that they are escaping.

Dead wrong. Fellas, listen up. She wants you to leave periodically. She and her network depend on it. Because that's when meetings are held. Sometimes they physically gather together, other times it's by phone or over the fence. Why do you think women always go to the bathroom as a group? Do you really think they're incapable of handling basic potty chores alone? Of course not. That's where they say things to each other that they can't say around their men. That's where strategies are discussed and finalized. That's the war room where battles are won and lost. What should men do? It's obvious – stop leaving them alone! Stop giving them opportunities to build a better louse trap. Take away their privacy and you take away their historic advantage. Giving up golf or bowling might be a small price to pay to finally level the playing field?

Nice in theory, perhaps, but sadly, gentlemen, it's already too late. Cutting off women's private time was only possible in the good old days before technology brought us the cell phone and the internet. Today meetings are held in the very air we breathe, continuously. For women today, life itself is one giant, nonstop, ongoing male-management meeting. They're held not in coffee shops or living rooms, but in cyberspace at places with names like *www.MenShouldBeShot.com* and *www.HomeSchooledHubbies. org* and *www.PutMenOutOfOurMisery.edu*. The pen may be mightier than the sword, but the modern mouse trumps them both, and today's proof is in the pixel. Her tiny fingers fly, the meeting is in session, and her man's fate is doomed.

And with cell phones, a wife today can get a colleague's counsel anywhere, anytime, in under a minute. If a battling man and wife today take time out for something so minor as him using the john, she'll be armed with new tactics before he's even washed his hands.

So it's never going to be a fair fight until men come together and organize, and since that's never going to happen, men will continue to battle against odds that make Custer's seem like a nailbiter. Without even knowing it, men are getting beaten at their own game. While we're blissfully watching the game, they're the ones calling a huddle.

Chapter 24

A Good Man Needs
Good Management

So, big boy, you're part of a new team now. You have a "better half" (which you apparently never had before) which means you're new and improved and bound for great and even greater things.

As we all know, an effective team does everything together, as a smooth-running unit. You and your better half are going to dream together, plan together, strive together, occasionally stumble together, but more often excel, shine, triumph and prosper together. You two will face many formidable challenges ahead, but they will be no match for solid teamwork.

But like any good teammates, you're going to have to communicate often and effectively.

And like any new teammates getting used to each other's habits and behavior, you must communicate in new ways as you transition from a solo act to a duet. No more "I"'s and "me"'s out of you, those days are over. From now on it's "we" did this and "we" went there and "we" don't close the bars and drink so much anymore.

Yes, Mr. Married Man, "we" is the new "me." "Me" was nice to have around, there's no denying, and he served you proudly and well for many long years. But when you said "I do", "me" rode into the sunset. "We" is the new sheriff in town, with "our" and "us" as his chief deputies. Your life-long buddies "I/me/mine" have been replaced by "we/our/us."

Alas, if it were only that simple. How easy life would be if all a freshly-married husband had to do was cut-and-paste "we/our/us" into his old sentences and be done with it. But it's so much more sophisticated than that.

Because "we" has always been a multifaceted word, and never more so than when referring to husband-and-wife. Remember when you first learned that the Royal "we" doesn't really mean "we" at all? Well the Royal "we" is child's play compared to the intricacy of the Marital "we." Children in grade school can master the Royal "we" in short order. But wrinkled old men, 75-year veterans of marriage, still struggle and are impaled on the spear tips of the Marital "we", so great are the depths of its complexity.

And that is because – and write this down, dummy – sometimes "we" means "we", but other times "we" means "you." And the hard part is it's the husband's job to know the difference.

There are no simple, universal rules, otherwise there would be no challenge. What "we/our/us" means in my marriage may not be the same for your marriage. There's no easy way around it – you'll have to learn as you go. It's live and learn, live and learn, live and learn, learn, learn, learn, learn.

Let's start off with an easy one. When I overhear Sarah say, "We wouldn't miss your niece's wedding for the world," I know that "we" was plural and that one of my future and perfectly glorious Saturday afternoons just went bye-bye. Not one woman in a thousand will attend a wedding alone, bank on it. So in that context, "we" means "we will be there," as well as "my husband will be the one with the expression like he's getting a rectal exam." And plan to kiss $100 good-bye, too. Place settings don't grow on trees, ya know.

On the other hand, Sarah and I were recently walking in our yard at home when she casually observed, "We need to spread more landscape chips." May-Day, red flag, Euphemism Alert! "We" in this context does not mean this is a job she and I are going to perform together.

Sarah does not do landscaping. Why? She would answer that question with a question. "Do you know what digging in the dirt would do to a $60 nail job?" I do not, but I have to assume it to be unspeakable.

Women's nails have evolved dramatically over the eons. Cavewomen used their nails to tear flesh from the bones of mastodons. Modern women's nails have become tiny canvases on which to display 10 or even 20 mini-Monet's. And it should go without saying, when you're wearing the Louvre on your extremities, you don't do chores that might ruin a masterpiece. I've come to understand this so well that the other day I bought Sarah a coffee cup which reads, "I Would Make Dinner But I Can't Find The Phone Book."

So I know from experience that "we need to spread more

landscape chips" means "I" need to drop by the nursery for a few bags of bark. It's the same general message if she should say any of the following:

"We should clean out the gutters."

"We ought to extend the deck."

"We must remodel the guest bath."

"We really have to paint the dining room."

"We need another coat of tar on the driveway."

Again, do not be fooled. None of these mean she's planning to pick up a paint brush, hammer, ladder or so much as a single leaf. And she's definitely not going to mess with those stinky, sticky driveway rollers. "We" means "you", big guy. She's done her job, which was to spot the problem. Your job, which still glaringly remains undone, is to fix it.

That's the division of responsibility in marriage. Wives are there to identify problems and supervise. Husbands are there to shut up and do the work.

To put it in terms any working man can understand:

She's Management – You're Labor.

(All marriages? No. Just mine and 97% of my brethren. The other 3% have guns, liquor, mullets and a willingness to serve time, so their homes run on a slightly different paradigm.)

Wives are management with white collars who see the big picture, plan, prepare, organize, strategize, prioritize, schedule, oversee, assign, delegate, document, budget, diagram, monitor, prod, poke, encourage, threaten and finalize.

Husbands are labor with blue collars who bend, lift, grunt, haul, tow, lug, heave, tote, shovel, carry, drag, scrape, push, pull, blister and bleed.

Simple, huh?

Women envision – men sweat.

Does this come as a shock to any of my fellow men?

Wasn't it a clue that it's called "MAN-agement" in the first place? It couldn't be a more basic organizational chart, could it?

As with all org charts, if you want to see who you report to, look up.

If you want to see who you need to watch like a hawk and who will find any excuse to goof off, look down.

So to recap in light of the chart, sometimes "we" means both management and labor will be working together, and sometimes "we" means management will send labor to do the heavy lifting.

There is one firm rule about "we" versus "I", however, and that is that plural sometimes means singular, but singular never means plural.

For instance, when Sarah says, "I was thinking we should refinish the hardwood floor," that only means that she (singular) was thinking we should refinish the hardwood floor.

It does not mean that I, her husband, was also thinking we should refinish the hardwood floor. Only her imagination was at work here. Mine, as usual, was disengaged.

But if she continues to mull it over for a few days and eventually says, "We're going to refinish the hardwood floor," that means "I" need to stop by the tool rental store and pick up an industrial sander, gloves, chemicals and dust mask and kiss off another perfectly glorious future Saturday.

Management has spoken, and for both of us.

Don't be discouraged, young new husbands, you'll get the hang of it. Being labor has its advantages. You don't have to think much, just take directions, it's honest work, none of the weighty responsibility of leadership, three squares a day, and you even get the occasional pat on the head.

Plus you get to sleep with the boss. And isn't access to power is almost as good as power itself?

Chapter 25

Understanding Women's Clothing Is Within Your Grasp - Unless Einstein's Theory Throws You

Sometimes the lesson that your wife has to teach you is that there is no point in administering the lesson in the first place, because, even with all your male powers plugged in and focused, you won't get it.

Such is the case with women's clothing and their alien size system.

I've tried, and I've seen other men try, but it's futile and hopeless. Sorry fellas, but we're never going to decode the mysterious, puzzling method women use to dress themselves.

It starts with the bra. Men can't even understand the everyday commercials we see on TV.

For example, we wonder, what happens if you wear an 18-hour bra for about a week?

That's our big question: What are the consequences of exceeding the time limit? Heaven only knows, but it can't be pretty.

That's Sarah's way of letting me know she's ready for a big day at the mall. She comes out of her dressing room and says, "Look out, world, I got on my 18-hour bra." To which I reply, "I gotcha beat, got on my seven-day shorts. Popped 'em on Tuesday, still goin' strong."

Also from the commercials, men don't know why a woman would even want a bra that will "lift and separate." Separate? Is that important? Tangled breasts a big problem for some women? Keeping them apart a big challenge? Are women really complaining to one another, "Will you just look at this mess? I just washed 'em and I can't do anything with 'em. I would give my left one just to know which one is my left one. I've got to get a filing system."

Even as boys, we males were confounded to learn that there was such a thing as a "training bra."

What?

"Training?"

Young boys jump to a lot of wrong conclusions here. Apparently, we imagine, when breasts are brand new, they can be very unruly. So it must be the case that you have to strap them in and teach 'em who's boss.

Apparently, like a new puppy, one must train them to "stay." It must be like growing roses, we suppose, in that you have to make sure to start them correctly, or they might come in crooked.

And who was the evil scientist who devised the illogical A-thru-D cup size scale?

Young boys attend school for years, striving to achieve, and it's deeply embedded into their heads that an "A" is a good thing and a "D" is a bad thing. Then, after years of learning and coming to understand that an "A" is better than a "B", which is better than a "C", which is better than a "D", along comes the bra world to say, "Time Out. New Rules. Everything you thought you knew is now exactly the opposite!"

Men have no experience with a scale where a D is better than an A. We're taught to shoot for A's, and to fear that a D might even be punishable.

Bring home an A, everybody screams for joy, you get a steak dinner. Bring home a D, they just scream, no dinner.

But then about the age of sixteen, most boys are strangely attracted to the lure of breasts, so much so that we want to learn the language and everything else about them. And with this first exposure to the universe of female clothing sizes, men learn that nothing we know is relevant, the rules are totally random and arbitrary, and we're up that same old creek without a paddle again. Because now men learn they are living in a world where one should be ashamed of a D in a classroom, but proud of a D in a sweater. And in fact, where sweaters are concerned, two D's are even better than one. They usually come that way, actually, in matching pairs.

(But beware, three is a problem. You can have too much of a good thing.)

Men like to believe they are good at logic. Men believe they are able to take a problem and think it through to a cold, calm, logical, rational solution. And when it comes to men's clothing sizes, that is indeed the case. Men's clothing sizes make sense. It's a simple system, and one can explain it to someone easily and within minutes. If a man's jacket is size 44, that means he's 44 inches around the chest. Size 36 pants means he's 36 inches around the waist. If a dress shirt is size 16-35, that means he's 16 inches around the neck and 35 inches down the sleeve. Simple, logical, explainable.

Man #1:
"What size does your wife wear?"

Man #2:
"Daaah, I don't know for sure. I think it's either ten . . . or petite, or junior, or 'W?' But I think I've heard ten a few times, so I'm goin' with ten."

Man #1:
"OK, ten what?"

Man #2:
"Daaah, I really dunno. Uh, ten . . . wait, I can get this. Gotta be somethin' simple, right, like ten, uh . . . femimeters? Ten units of woman? Ten . . . lady pieces? I just know that a tiny little woman is a two, so I guess she's five times bigger than that?

"Does that sound right?

"No, probably not, and I'm sorry."

I found by asking hundreds of men that most believe size two is as low as her sizes get, because that's the smallest size they've accidentally overheard in a conversation.

Many men are surprised to learn there is actually a size one, and they're positively floored when they learn that below a one, there really is a – drumroll, please – size ZERO! Try it at home. Drop that info on a man and watch his face. It's good, quality fun.

"Are you kiddin'? There's a ZERO?"

Yes, gentlemen, it is in fact the dream of some women to walk into a dress shop and say, "I'd like to see something in a nothing. I'm not a two, not a one. No, I'm a none. It's a curse, I can't help it, but I am just tooooo tiny for positive numbers."

And gents, in their dreamiest of dream worlds, they'd try on a zero . . . and it's too baggy. Now she needs something from the minus-negative part of the shop.

But no, while dresses do not descend into negative numbers, believe it or not, there is a size lower than zero, and it is – double drumroll, please – DOUBLE ZERO. Double zero is even smaller than zero.

Yes, my confused male friends, this is completely mathematically illogical, seemingly impossible. School taught us all that zero multiplied by anything is still just plain old zero.

But women can improve upon anything, even immutable laws of mathematics. For in their world, zero can be doubled and result in something even teensier.

Want to know the difference between a zero and a double zero? A zero ate a carrot last week. A double zero saw a picture of a carrot last year.

Size double zero was invented because women are secretly yet fiercely competitive, so they have double zero in the hope that if they can ever fit into one, then they could stand next to a mere zero and say, "Pig."

(What does a double zero have in common with a vampire? Neither one casts a shadow.)

Men wonder whether there is a size smaller than double zero, maybe triple zero? The answer is no, because the only humans smaller than double zero are embryos, and they don't need clothes because they live in isolated nudist colonies for three-quarters of their first year.

Women's accessories are just as puzzling. Women will actually buy and wear a tight little belt for the neck, which is blatantly and explicitly called – ready? – a "choker." No man would go near a device which tells you right up front that it's a choker. To a man, a choker is a wrestling hold, and potentially fatal. It's so dangerous it's illegal, so you have the comfort of knowing that if your opponent uses it, he'll be disqualified, and you'll be declared the winner. Posthumously, but congratulations all the same. You added one to the wins column and the undertaker added one to the cemetery.

But women will voluntarily, and with their own hands, put

something called a choker around their necks. Apparently the drive to accessorize is so strong that women are willing to risk oxygen-deprivation to achieve it.

Is it possible that women endure this torture just to obtain the company of men? I asked Sarah, who suggested I consider the possibility that a little oxygen-deprivation makes the company of men more tolerable.

Learn also, men, that women hate it when we try to use logic on them. For example, Sarah started saying she wanted a tennis bracelet.

My reply, "I think we should get you a racket first. Let's see how you like the game before we buy the uniform?"

The lesson? Don't use logic. Trust me, you'll be sorry.

- Female Football -
Civil Turf Wars Come Out Of The Closet

Men, when we retreat into our little world of football, we think we're escaping to a place where women won't follow, because they don't understand, live and love the game like we do.

What men often fail to grasp is that women not only understand the concept behind football, but are masters of it. In fact, they use it against us every day, and we don't even know it. This is because marriage is, and has always been, about ground-gaining and land acquisition. Two people, but only one house to divide between them. Can you feel the tension and suspense? Then let's suit up and get this bowl game under way.

The whistle to start the game blows the minute the new couple moves into their first house. But the problem is it's on an extreme frequency well beyond the range of man-made instruments, which means only women can hear it. Therefore, the new husband is oblivious to the fact that the game is even under way. He's often at the concession stand looking for a brat and a beer, blissfully ignorant that she's racking up points against a defense that's not even on the field. Heck, you don't even need to be a good team to score against an opponent who hasn't even pulled his jock on, right?

167

Make no mistake, gentlemen, your house in an ongoing gridiron battle, whether you recognize it or not. Because the object of both marriage and football lies in fighting for, claiming and occupying your opponent's territory. When a wife "gains ground", it's around the house, not on the football field, but it's every bit as hard-fought and competitive, the result of careful planning, practice and execution. Like every great competitor, she analyzes her opponent's strengths (right!) and weaknesses, learns his habits, then pounces when he least expects it and where he is the most poorly defended. And once she acquires a piece of territory, look out, because she never, never, never, never gives it back.

Sarah is the perfect example. She's resourceful, savvy, ruthless, shrewd, and can map out a game plan to rival Lombardi, Shula and Noll combined. Sarah actually took a beautiful, spacious, huge his-and-her walk-in closet and converted it . . . to a "HER." This closet is bigger than my first apartment, and not one thing in there is mine. This is a room that should be adequate to house clothing for ten and still have space left over for a grand piano and a chest freezer. But not so much as one sock in that suite belongs to me.

That's something about men that fascinates me endlessly, that a man can maintain his illusion of superiority when she's annexed the entire closet, while he's left with two doorknobs on the guest room. Or his stuff's in a refrigerator crate down by the furnace. He's changing clothes on a cold concrete floor, muttering to himself, "But I'm the king of this castle, by golly." Sure you are, Captain Delusion.

Closet displacement is usually the first place that the new husband senses he's being "man"-ipulated like so much furniture, but it's not the last. Quietly and gradually, Sarah has taken over most of the square footage of our house. Learn this lesson well, new husbands:

Your wife is there primarily to colonize the house.

Wives are like pilgrims. They arrive, smile, show courtesy and bring food. They seem friendly enough. But make no mistake, they have an unspoken agenda. Eventually they acquire one piece of territory, then another, then another, until the husband is pushed off onto a tiny, primitive, comfortless, resource-starved reservation known as the garage.

Inside one year of marriage, my dear young husband friends, know and expect that the garage will be all you'll have left of your "kingdom." Her part of the house has carpet, curtains, potpourri, grace, ambience, mood lighting and lace. Your part doesn't even have drywall or heat.

And when the husband is in her part of the house, there's still the question of decorating, yet another language men don't speak. The reason, I learned, is because men are deaf. It turns out a house also makes sounds only a woman can hear, just like the whistle that started the game he doesn't know he's in.

Houses, I now understand, speak to women. Houses do not speak to men.

I first became aware of this one day when I arrived home to find we had an entire brand new dining room set. Thousands of dollars I would not have spent, but that's because I am house-deaf, as are most men. But relax, fellas, it's not that bad. House-deafness is not as extreme a disability as normal deafness. You can still hear everything except HGTV and Martha Stewart.

Sarah informed me that in fact the house was, in her words, "screaming" for new dining room furniture. Screaming? I said, "Our house was screaming?" Apparently our house belongs in a Steven King novel. I asked, "Why didn't I hear all the screaming?" Sarah said she didn't know, but fortunately, she heard it distinctly enough for both of us. And, just as fortunately, with the purchase of this furniture, she had made the house happy again and, for the moment, it had stopped screaming.

She explained that houses scream for things when they detect that the overall composition of the domestic landscape is out of balance. One house might scream for a new sunroom, another for designer drapes, yet another for a remodeled bathroom. Sarah assured me that houses only scream when absolutely necessary, and they are to be heeded. Our house was screaming because our old dining room set no longer fit in.

Naturally, I had to ask, if the house was screaming so loud, why hadn't someone else heard it? Surely a neighbor, the mailman, a pedestrian, someone would have heard the horrible screaming and brought it to my attention, if only to reestablish peace and quiet in the neighborhood. Sarah explained that, indeed, other wives were aware of the screaming, a meeting was held, and they had collaborated on a team effort to get the house what it needed so it could be at peace again. For the time being, I was told, my house was not screaming for anything. Not that I would know, because to my ears it turns out a happy house and a screaming house sound exactly alike. (Both make about as much noise to my ears as my pet turtle, George, who died 49 years ago.) But Sarah assures me not to worry about it, because she and her friends will take prompt action when – not if – the screaming returns.

So decorating is best left to the wife, because men just don't get it. But a warning to new husbands, even if you want to be part of a decorating decision, be prepared to be ignored and defeated. In fact, all your participation can realistically achieve is to slow down the process.

On those rare occasions when I do visit the furniture store with Sarah, we never agree on what to get. I tend to pick louder, more flamboyant pieces, as do many men, I understand. But Sarah always tells me we should go with more conservative items, often in "earth tones." Again the language barrier rears its ugly head. "Earth tones?", I ask. "You mean, like dirt? When I have earth tones on my shoes, you won't let me in the house. Now all of a sudden we're going to drop big money for colors we pay Stanley Steemer to remove?"

But Sarah will hear none of it – suddenly she's selectively deaf – opting for earth tones, and explaining that we shouldn't get my brassier choice because, in her words, "We'd get tired of it." To which I respond, "Great. Let's get what you want, and we can be tired of it instantly. My way, at least we get a month of fun. With earth tones, we don't even get that, because they left the fun out of it at the factory."

The session ends, cash registers ring, I wave good-bye to the chair I wanted, and we go home to await the delivery of more earth tones. That home may be your castle, fella. But it's her canvas, and you don't get a brush.

Chapter 27

When "I'm Sorry" Is Not Enough

Make no mistake, "I'm sorry" works better than any other words mankind has yet devised to tame the angered female. Unfortunately, even after the male apology has been offered and accepted, many times she's still not finished. Which means, fella, that you're not finished.

To a man's eternal bewilderment, she often still wants to know "Why?" As in, "Why did you do that in the first place?"

The reason men are bewildered is because it would not occur to a man to ask such a question after an apology, because between men, an apology ends all discussion. Period. You're sorry, I accept, argument over, let's have a beer. And for that matter, what argument? That's how fast the issue becomes ancient history between males.

But not to your wife, you dumb stud biscuit. To her, while an apology is a necessary step toward restoring good relations and domestic harmony, there is still grist for the conversational mill to be found, bound and ground. More talk is in order, for two reasons. First, she doesn't want this to happen again, Mr. Buns-For-Brains, so let's nip any future acts of stupidity squarely in the bud. And second, as hopeless as it may seem, she still aspires to one day figure out exactly how it is your mindless mind works.

So she needs to know why you were such an idiot. And she has no one else to ask but you. So strap in, big guy, you're in for a bumpy ride.

"Why did you use our good guest towels to wash the car?"

"Why did you try to defrost the turkey in the dryer?"

"Why did you let the kids fingerpaint in the den with the new carpet?"

"Why did your brain tell you that a sheet of newspaper would make a good coffee filter?"

"Why don't you ever listen instead of doing everything your way?"

"Why don't you drop dead?"

No matter what else you might say or think, gentlemen, you have to give women credit for being voraciously, intensely, insatiably, insanely curious creatures. Why, why, why, why, why, why, why, why, why, why? Women are round-the-clock Columbo's hot on the trail of the cause of your latest boneheaded "man"-euver. Turns out science only got it half right. Men may possess the Y chromosome. But women carry the far more dangerous and deadly "WHY?" chromosome.

So what's a man to do? You blew it, you apologized, you were even sincere, but still she wants to know "Why?" As in, for example, "Why did you eat the pecan pie I made for company? What were you thinking?"

You can't tell her the truth, which would be, "I wasn't thinking at all. I seldom do. I was reacting, like a lion reacts to a zebra. It was there, it was within my reach, in the blink of an eye it was in my hands, and by the second blink, it was history. It was a pecan pie, and you know I cannot resist pecan pie. Once I get that first taste, the only thing that can stop me is the bottom of the pan. If you can't fault a lion for being a lion, then you can't fault me for being me. I cannot tell a lie, I ate the pie and the zebra, I loved every tender bite, and I'd do it again! Besides, it's your fault for leaving it where I could get at it in the first place."

While all that may be a perfectly accurate reason why the pie went the way of the zebra, you absolutely cannot utter that explanation to your wife. It's too long, too involved, and gives her way too many new opportunities to launch an overwhelming second round of new questions, like:

"Why weren't you thinking about my feelings and all the hard work I put into that dessert?"

"Why weren't you thinking about our company?"

"Why couldn't you have waited to ask me if it was OK to dig your dirty paws into the pie?"

"Why can't you ever exercise a little self-control?"

"Why do you only think about yourself and your needs?"

"Why can't you set a better example for the children?"

"What gives you the nerve to think you have anything in common with a lion?"

Every explanation you might offer is just one more chance for her to load another "Why?" into the chamber and fire it back in your face. It's a game you'll never win and you're a fool to even play. What you really need most is the Husband's Secret Weapon, and the majority of your fellow men had to learn this the hard way, through experience and after years of futility. But here it is, offered to you in order to deliver you from 40 long years of aimlessly wandering the marital desert without a compass:

When you're backed into a corner, nothing works like ignorance.

That's right, pleading ignorance is the husband's equivalent of Monopoly's Get-Out-Of-Jail-Free card. It works in virtually every situation.

Its two main strengths are, first, she's stuck for a comeback. After all, how do you ask a man, "Why were you ignorant?" But second, and most importantly, male ignorance is so completely believable to your wife.

But how to express it in the most convincing manner, that's the real question. The best approach, like most things in life, is pure, short and sweet. It's one word, six simple syllables. And though it will require practice for new husbands to be able to deliver effectively, it is more than worth the effort. Here's the word, the result of generations of collective male experience:

"IONONOBEDDER"

I know it looks foreign, but that's just at first blush. It's perfect English, and it's perfectly effective, once you get its meaning and feel its power. Try saying it slowly at first, over and over, feeling its subtlety, motion and momentum, again and again. After about a dozen repetitions, you'll get the rhythm and its glory will unfold before you. You'll say, "Of course, now I see. IONONOBEDDER. Brilliant. And the best part is, I really don't. It's not only the perfect alibi, it's also the truth!"

"IONONOBEDDER" works in places where even the most logically sound reply on earth would fall flat. It just plain stops her cold. You're admitting you have no experience or training in the matter at hand to fall back on, so by implication whatever you did was the best-guess stab in the dark of a rudderless slob just trying to get through life the best he can with his good intentions and gut instincts.

Just for safe measure, in order to really sell it, always say it with a sad-eyed, Basset Hound look on your face. That way, if your ignorance doesn't break through her defenses, your hang-dog face should engage her maternal/protective/nurturing side and push it over the edge.

So practice, practice, practice. Sad eyes, helpless expression, and a sincere, "IONONOBEDDER." Rehearse till it's perfect, then put it on the shelf, and pull it out only when life, marriage and the woman of your dreams offer you no other option. But when, not if, you find yourself in that dreaded corner, pull it down, give it your best Oscar-worthy delivery, and watch it work its magic.

"Why did you bring home bourbon and chips when I sent you to the store for vacuum cleaner bags?"

"IONONOBEDDER."

"Why did you buy a new boat when you knew we needed to remodel the bathroom?"

"IONONOBEDDER."

"Why did you moon my mother at the breakfast table?"

"IONONOBEDDER?"

It's simple, it's elegant, it's efficient and it's beautiful. And in the right hands, it can save you literally years of work and wasted energy. Using only this single technique plus $750, a new husband can ensure, in the very first week after the ceremony, that we will never have to do laundry again for the duration of his marriage. Sound too good to be true? Here's how:

Gentlemen, eagerly volunteer to do the first load of wash as soon as you get back from the honeymoon. After the machine has run its cycle, call your wife into the laundry room, show the tattered wet load of clothes to your new wife and apologize. Explain to her tenderly that, "It was an honest mistake. After all, the drain cleaner was sitting right next to the detergent, and the bottles look so much alike . . . and . . . well . . ."

A new washing machine costs $500, and an average load of ruined clothes runs about $250. Total out-of-pocket: $750. A truly small price to pay to never have to do a load of wash again. And the longer you stay married, the lower the annual expense. By your golden anniversary, it'll be down to a modest fifteen dollars a year. What an incredible bargain, and a sound investment in your future.

And all you have to do is know what to say when she asks, "Why couldn't you read the label, you big moron?"

Lay it on her, fella. Let her have it, with both barrels, right between the "Why""s. Wearing your best "Dumb & Dumber" face.

"IONONOBEDDER."

You're welcome. My little gift to you.

Chapter 28

A Rose, By Any Other Name, Can Make It All Right Again

Every man in the history of men has screwed up and needs to know what to do to get back in her good graces and beyond. (Let's face it, "beyond" is important, because good graces may be nice, but they don't curl your toes and make you forget your own name. Men don't want only to be forgiven. They're hoping to make it to the great "beyond.")

You might think there are some men so virtuous, considerate and thoughtful that they've never blundered into the "Land of the Unforgiven." Men who've never had to dirty their knees begging for redemption. Mythical, godlike men who never had to beg for mercy in Her Highness's Court.

But you'd be wrong.

Every man – repeat, *every man* – has either found or will find himself in that position, no matter how gracious his demeanor might seem. Dr. Phil? Sure. Alan Alda? No question. Paul Newman? Are you kidding? Mr. Newman, by his own account, when he was 80 years old, bummed cigarettes from an extra on a movie set, then begged the beggee, "Do me a favor. Don't tell my wife you gave these to me." Butch Cassidy wouldn't be afraid of a woman if he wasn't haunted by bad experiences from crossing her in the past. And if a woman can scare Butch Cassidy, then honestly, what chance do you have?

So certain is it that every man will eventually find himself on her bad side that Hallmark has pre-written an entire series of cards for when – not if – it happens. Hallmark literally bets on the fallibility of men, and prepares a product male offenders can buy when – not if – the offense occurs.

Hallmark is cocked, loaded and ready to profit from each and every male who makes a wrong move. If no man screws up, Hallmark would have to eat all those cards. They'd lose a bundle. But instead they're poised to make – and do make – a fortune because you cannot lose betting against good collective male behavior.

Hallmark's biggest annual sales event, of course, is Valentine's Day, named after the Roman priest who, around 270 A.D., defied Emperor Claudius the Second and performed marriage ceremonies despite the fact Claudius had outlawed them. Claudius was not amused, and Valentine eventually lost 10 inches of stature which had previously been his head. But what Valentine lacked in height he made up for in holiness, became a saint, and centuries later we continue to celebrate his brave acts in furtherance of sweet love every February 14.

Which, I believe, raises the need for a new Hallmark holiday on February 13. It turns out many men today use Valentine's Day as a general apology day for any sins committed in the weeks or months leading up to the day. As a result, many men find themselves in a goodwill deficit position coming into Valentine's

Day, and use their gifts and cards on February 14 just to get back to even. And if one has only made it back to even, it can be difficult to attain the "beyond."

Therefore, I propose that February 13 should be National "I'm Sorry" Day. This would be a countrywide, CARD-ONLY day of male atonement, when forgiveness is sought for anything which might dampen the mood on Valentine's Day proper. No gifts!! They come the next day, always have, and it's expensive enough the way it is. February 13 would be a $4.95 occasion at most, with the emphasis not on the material, but the emotional component of being cleansed, renewed, refreshed, redeemed and forgiven.

Yes, I can imagine some of the women crying, "What? No gift? What kind of a romantic holiday comes with no gift?" Ladies. Please. Can't you wait just 24 hours? Just one more sunrise? One lousy rotation of the Earth. St. Valentine didn't defy Rome and die in vain. Gifts will come tomorrow. Do you know how close that is? It's already tomorrow in Japan. Please, think of it as one more card than you otherwise were going to get this year, accept his gesture and apology, erase the ledger, reset his account to zero, and hit February 14th with spirits high. And if the night of the 14th gets here and he still hasn't come through, there'll still be plenty of time to plan his painful and torturous demise.

But even if we successfully establish this new holiday, no single national day of "Sorry" will eliminate the need for men to continue apologizing from time to time. Some mistakes are so big they can't be put on the shelf to fester until next February. Some mistakes must be apologized for – and NOW. Otherwise he might not make it to next February. So men will always need to know how to apologize, and they should be prepared to act quickly and in the most appropriate and effective way.

In my standup career, I have asked many audiences, "When a husband messes up, traditionally, what should he buy for his wife as an apology gift?" The overwhelmingly majority answer is always flowers. Yes, a few say diamonds, but we're talking working people here, so flowers it is. I follow up and ask, "If it's flowers, then specifically, what kind of flowers?" And always the loud, unanimous voice of every crowd cries back, "Roses."

It's a jarringly simple voice to hear. There is never any dissent. Diverse audiences, from all over the country, even all over the world, vastly different walks of life, and with no preparation or rehearsal, they thunder out with a forceful, authoritative, single voice, "Roses."

It's as though they're saying, "Hey, we're not stupid. We know the score. You go to the store, you get roses, you go home, hold 'em out, and you say, 'I'm sorry.'"

That is in fact why there are over 30,000 flower shops in the U.S. Three reasons, really. Weddings, funerals and "I'm sorry."

But ask an audience, on the other hand, "When a wife wishes to apologize to her husband, traditionally, what should she buy for him?" and a most awkward, strange-yet-amused silence falls over a crowd. Give them more time, lots more time, but still no answer will come. Then finally the magical music of laughter when they're asked, "Do you feel the confusion?"

The laughter flows freely then. Because they recognize, based on the reality their own lives, that there is no traditional gift for a wife who has messed up to buy for her husband. And why not? Because apparently women don't mess up often enough for there to be a tradition.

To have a tradition, one must have frequency, meaning it must happen a lot. Men screw up constantly, and we have developed roses as our tradition. On the other hand, the average woman only messes up 3-4 times in her whole life (I think it's in the by-laws), and that is not enough for a tradition to take root.

An unexpected by-product of this line of inquiry is that women will regularly respond with, "No, you don't buy him anything. You know what you do!" Which is said while rolling the eyes seductively to indicate that wifely apologizing involves activity above and "beyond."

To which I can only say: Fellas, stop and think about that concept, if you can possibly get your head around it. Sex . . . as an APOLOGY? Stunning. Truly mindblowing. Women, all we men want to know is how did you get there? And when can we men ever hope to catch up?

When can we men hope for the day when we can come to you and say, "Sweetheart? I just feel so bad about what I did. All I want in the world is for you to forgive me. And, well, if you have to . . . TAKE ME NOW. Show no mercy, honey, I was bad, MAKE ME SORRY!"

Don't hold your breath, fellas.

The Red-Eye From Venus Must Have Been A Killer

Despite the fact that we're wired differently, and the barriers to total understanding may even be insurmountable, both sides keep trying to figure out the other, and we've spawned an impressive pile of theories. Some say our behaviors come from genetics; others say it's all learned. Some say it's basic animal instinct; others say it's environmental. Some trace its roots to prehistoric times; others credit modern phenomena.

A popular '90's theory went so far as to say it's due to the solar system. Dr. John Gray wrote a book titled "Men Are From Mars, Women Are From Venus", and sold over 24 million copies. 24 million people bought this book. Could there possibly be any greater proof that we will never understand each other than the fact that a man could write a book, the title of which is "Men Are From Mars, Women Are From Venus," and 24 million people would reach for their money, thinking, "That just might be it! Maybe men are from Mars, waaay over here. And maybe women are from Venus, waaay over there. Sure. Finally, something that makes sense. Here I was limiting myself to single-planet thinking, and all the while the answer was out there in the cosmos. That must be it. Ya gotta think outside the globe!"

24 million people so earnestly desperate for answers that they parted with twenty bucks in the hope that maybe, just maybe, they'd understand the opposite sex better by learning more about their planet of origin. These are people who've been muttering to themselves for years that there's no way their partner could have been raised in this world. And along comes John Gray, who says that none of us are truly from here. He says men and women were actually born and raised on completely different planets, then at some age are transported here to this neutral territory, where it's no wonder they have trouble getting along because they're dealing with some of the negative effects of forced inter-galactic bussing. They've both been ripped from their natural environments and forced to coexist with other creatures of vastly different backgrounds. And while they may learn to get along as time goes by, as that old saying goes, you can take the boy out of Mars, but you can't take Mars out of the boy.

Which is not to dismiss the Mars/Venus theory in the least. Maybe there's something to it. Perhaps men are from Mars. After all, it's the Red Planet – the angry, surly, vengeful, probably constipated planet – distant, hostile, named after the Roman god of war. Maybe that's why men are such macho buttheads all the time.

And possibly women are from Venus. It's the most beautiful, most mysterious planet. It's the Morning Star, the Evening Star, it's named after the goddess of beauty and love. It also happens to be the gassy planet. Not that it's wise to bring it up. Women can be a little defensive about that.

One day when Sarah was less than delighted with me, she threatened to write her own book, "Women Are From Venus, Men Are A Pain In The Ass!" Then, just in case the first book left any unanswered questions, maybe a sequel, "Men Are From Mars, And They Should Go Back Where They Came From."

In defense of men, it's important to point out one overlooked fact about the Mars/Venus controversy. Venus is 26 million miles from Earth, so that's how far feminine space-travelers had to come to join the Great Dance. But Mars is 35 million miles from Earth. Which means each man traveled 9 million extra miles for the privilege of getting his name on her dance card. You can fault man's insight, depth, thoughtfulness, understanding, empathy or compassion, but you cannot deny the incontrovertible fact that man put in a 35% greater effort just to be here. Win or lose, men wouldn't have missed this for the world, let alone permit a measly 9 million additional miles to stand in their way.

26 million miles for woman. 35 million miles for man. 61 million miles between them. And you thought salmon traveled a long way to mate!

By contrast, scientists estimate that when Santa Clause flies to every rooftop on Christmas morning to deliver presents, he travels a mere 1,360,000 miles. Wimp.

(As an aside, and as a minor item of pride, I would like to point out that this entire discussion of the solar system was completed without a single cheap joke about Uranus. Butt I digress.)

All The Answers Are Hanging On The Bathroom Wall

Men and women. So what does it all boil down to? What do I think I've learned about men and women from fifty-five trips around the sun? Just this.

Men love efficiency.

Women love beauty.

I hear you. "Really? That's it? The whole thing is that simple? Come on. After all the millions of years of human gender interaction, it all comes down to efficiency versus beauty?"

To which I can only reply that it does not explain everything, only most of what's important. Please, take a little ride with me, and see if you agree.

First, men are motivated by efficiency because most men's lives are, indeed, a quest for ever-greater efficiency. In many households, even as we grow from boys into men, it's our job to get things done. Most men grow up being expected to build, repair, mend, adjust, fix, rig, restore, wire, patch and paint things. It's our job, often not a fun one, but a role we're expected to fulfill before we can move on to our favorite pursuits – recreation and leisure.

But in order to goof off, men are first expected to produce helpful results around the castle. So, naturally, men are attracted and motivated by any machine or device which hastens those results and speeds him on his way to the lake, ballpark, race track, arena, pub, stadium or golf course. Men get excited by devices which do what they say they will and do them quickly with no wasted time or motion. It's not that men enjoy the chore, but more that men crave the moment when the chore is done.

It is, in fact, because men are so into practicality and efficiency that one of the oldest battles between men and women continues to rage, that being that He always wants to drink milk straight from the carton right out of the fridge, while She, much more into elegance and aesthetics, wants her man to pour the milk first into a cut crystal glass, then drink it.

Men see no reason for the unnecessary middle step, and have precedent no further away than the garage to back their argument. When the lawn mower needs gas, what do we do? That's right, we pour gas straight from the gas can directly into the mower tank. That way the gas goes from where it is to where we want it to be in one perfect motion, no wasted effort, and no intermediate vessel gets dirtied in the process. Would it not be pointless to first pour the gas into a bone china gravy boat before putting it into the mower? What a silly, unnecessary step. Plus, who's got time to clean a gravy boat every time the grass needs cut?

Same with the milk. It's in the carton now, and we want it down our throats. So that's where we pour it. No muss, no fuss, no waste and nothing for the dishwasher. Hey, when the hotel wants us to use our towels again and again, they post a sign explaining it's good for the environment. Similarly, when men drink straight from the carton, we're saving soap, hot water, time and energy. So fellas, next time you're caught with your lips around the milk bottle, just say, "Honey, I'm not a slob. I'm being green! Just doin' my little part to save the planet."

The same division exists on the subject of wrist watches. Men's watch faces are big and bold and you can tell the time with the quickest of glances, often from across the room. But women's? Just the opposite. In fact, men will never understand why women encourage jewelers to make watches with tiny, blank, bald faces. Many women's watches have faces smaller than a fingernail and no markings on them of any kind at all. Just two tiny hands, no numbers whatsoever, not even tiny dots or scratches, nothing at all on the face for guidance.

So ask a man what time it is, and he will state authoritatively, "It's 12:48." But instead ask the woman next to him the same question, and she will stare curiously at her wrist, forefinger in mouth, and finally say, "Ummm, I'm not sure. I think, maybe, in 5 or 10 minutes it'll be either 1 or 2 o'clock? Sorry but that's the best I can do. Will that help you catch your plane?"

So there you have it. Men are hopelessly into efficiency. Women, on the other hand, while they may value efficiency, are inspired more by beauty and things which feed the soul. That is the only possible explanation why, in this day and age, one can still find candle stores.

There is not a man alive who understands why there are still candles for sale, let alone why there are entire stores – thousands of them – whose sole inventory consists of candles. To a man's utilitarian mind, candles in this day and age simply make no sense. Candles are unnecessary in a modern world. They have been far surpassed in efficiency by more recent strokes of genius.

A modern light bulb may have the light of a thousand candles. In fact, that's how the brightness of light bulbs is measured and expressed – in "candlepower." A modern furnace has the heat of a million candles. Wow! To a man's way of thinking, with efficiency like that available, why would anyone ever choose to fool around with one candle at a time? Men don't understand why something whose useful time has passed has not gone the way of the buggy whip. Why didn't Thomas Alva Edison end the Age of Candles?

But women have patiently explained to me that they fervently value the beauty, aroma, atmosphere, aura, even the soul of a single burning candle. And that is why candle stores still exist, and that is Sarah's place at the mall.

The man's place is the bench in the middle of the mall.

The mall bench, I've learned, is where husbands sit with all the other husbands. There's never been a woman sitting on the mall bench with us. It's just one, big, sit-down stag party. It's the mall's version of limbo, an arid no-woman's land, and should probably be officially named the "Bored Captive Husbands Day Care Center." Just for variety, it would surely be fun someday to see one woman sitting on one mall bench somewhere in the USA, crying out, "Fred's trying on pants, this could take all day."

It is in fact women's love of beauty which is partly responsible for the controversy surrounding the Augusta National Golf Club's policy of all-male membership. Women have been arguing for years that Augusta National should admit female members. And Augusta National has only itself to blame for the fuss.

Men have organized and maintained male-only clubs for centuries, usually without any female interference. These clubs generally involve male activities and are held in environs only men would frequent, such as the Every-Other-Thursday-Night-In-Hank's-Greasy-Garage-On-Mulberry-Street-In-South-Piscataway-New-Jersey-Poker-And-Cigar-Club, where women are openly, loudly, blatantly and expressly forbidden.

But they don't care. Because they've seen Hank's greasy garage, and no self-respecting woman would want to pass time there. It's just as disgusting as it sounds.

And in the old days, many years ago, Augusta National was just like Hank's garage. It was, in the beginning, plainly and simply a pleasant golf course where men could escape from their wives and just be men.

But then Augusta National blew it. They just could not leave well enough alone. They planted flowers.

Just a few at first, but soon more, many more. Magnificent shrubs, bushes, azaleas, magnolias, honeysuckle, lilacs, tulips and roses. In short, they made it beautiful. They made it one of the most gorgeous places in all the world. And that's what began the outcry that the walls must come a-tumbling down.

If they had kept it simple and dumpy, women may have never noticed and there would still be peace today. But plant too many flowers, make it attractive and aromatic, and you're going to draw in women like moths to a Gucci flame.

"Field of Dreams" was all about "If you build it, they will come." The lesson of Augusta National – "If you build it pretty, they will come, and they will want in."

And if you need final proof of which gender is more concerned with beauty, just ask yourself which one frequents a place called the "beauty shop."

So there it is. Men prize efficiency, and women prize beauty. And you do not have to look any further to see these two competing philosophies living side by side than your standard, everyday bath towel.

It's hanging right there on the rod in your bathroom. Most of what there is to know about men and women, draped in plain view right there next to the sink.

Because your normal bath towel is composed of a male part and a female part. They exist side by side, each different but each making its contribution to the whole, finding a way to overcome obstacles and work together in peace for the common good.

The male portion of the towel, of course, is the big, fluffy terrycloth part in the center of the towel. This is the male part, naturally, because it is so remarkably efficient. This part of the towel is soft, thirsty, absorbent, and it literally sucks up the water. A person can dry oneself with the male portion of the towel. And that is what we men foolishly thought a towel was supposed to do.

But then there are the female portions of the towel. These are, of course, the decorative strips at each end of the towel. And to the women of the world, no matter how pretty you may think these additions are, even you must admit that these deco-bands are useless to the main purpose of the towel, which is, or at least should be, to eliminate moisture.

But that is not possible with the female part of the towel, because these flowery end pieces are hard, and flat, and matted, but most mysteriously, *they repel water!* What? They're part of a towel. But they repel water? Test it. Lay the towel flat on a table and pour water on it. The water will soak rapidly into the male part and bead up on the female part. This is not just failure of a component to do its job. This is counter-efficient engineering intentionally inserted on the drawing board. To a man, this is a planned crash even before they wave the starting flag.

Men simply do not know what to make of the deco-bands. If the whole towel was made out of this, it wouldn't be a towel, it would be a placemat. Would you want to try to dry yourself after a shower with a placemat? Probably not. Yet somewhere at the factory, they took two slices of placemat, and they sewed them into my towel.

To a man's way of thinking, this part of the towel has no business being part of a towel. It would be like having underwear made out of mostly cotton, but a little ice cream.

Women say, "But they're decorative towels." But men think those two words should not be allowed to go together. Men believe there should be towels, and there should be decorations, but the two should never be combined.

And beyond just being inefficient, these deco-bands can actually hurt. You can nick yourself with this part of the towel. So gentlemen, next time you're drying with the family linens and these nasty strips of sandpaper scrape you in a sensitive area, just think of it as a friendly little "hello" from your wife, offered in the name of art, and for the sake of beauty.

A male aside to the wives: Sandpaper has its place, just not in the bathroom. Sandpaper is good when you're refinishing the deck. Sandpaper is bad when you're trying to dry off your tender tushy.

Indeed, men ask why fully 20% of every towel must be sacrificed so there can be beauty in the bathroom. To a man, this is valuable towel area that we could use to get 20% drier, 20% faster. And that is important to men because most of us are at least 20% bigger!

Men would say, if there must be beauty in the bathroom near the towel rod, please, by all means, buy a painting. Hang it on the wall right above the rod on which hangs a 100% plain terrycloth towel. Then literally everyone would be happy. Visitors to your bathroom would have beauty when they look in that direction, and your husband would not resent the painting because he would not have to dry himself with it.

Gentlemen of the world, if we decided to unite, we could mount a campaign and try to get rid of the irrational decorative towel strip. We could use logic and reason and try to win women over and eliminate this inefficient little demon. I campaigned for male causes with the women in my life when I was totally, absolutely, thoroughly, hopelessly young. I was naive, I was idealistic, but mostly, I was fatally young.

Yes, I was a young man once. It didn't work out.

But I fought hard for male causes. I fought valiantly with my Sarah, at least I thought I did. But in the end I had to admit I seldom won her over to my way of thinking. She is a formidable adversary, as are most in her Sisterhood.

So, gentlemen, I close and bid you well by saying to you that women are the reason for many, many things in the world, and I ask you to find it in your heart to appreciate, learn from, and even love what they bring to the table.

For there truly are so many fine and wondrous lessons you can learn from your wife.

For women are the reason for pumps and clogs and flats and slings, periwinkle and seafoam, size zero, candle stores and decorative linens. And they are the reason for millions of other both greater and lesser things, all of which add texture, interest, beauty, mystery and magic to the fabric of life.

So, gentlemen, when you're tempted to take these women on, and challenge the feminine influences in the world, by all means do what's in your heart. But my advice, use your head, save a lot of time, add literally years to your life, and about nine out of ten times, be a very wise man:

Throw in the towel.

I Almost Forgot

Always remember that communication is the key to a successful marriage. The experts say it so often it's become trite, but it's nonetheless true. Sometimes, gentlemen, you can go by what she says. Other times, you need to read between the lines. In my own case, recently I was standing in my kitchen, and Sarah came up behind me and grabbed me by the seat of the pants. And I thought, "Hey! That's gotta be a good thing."

Turns out my little darlin' was just drying her hands.

You see, fellas, that's what marriage is all about.

Sometimes it's your job to understand and make peace with the towel.

And other times it's your job to be the towel.